PROFIT-RICH SALES FOR LENDERS, BROKERS, AND PRIVATE BANKERS

THE PROVEN SECRETS GUARANTEED TO CLOSE MORE DEALS AT PREMIUM PRICING

ROXANNE EMMERICH
TERRY SLATTERY

Banner Press

BANNER PRESS
MINNEAPOLIS, MN

Printed in the United States of America
Publisher: Banner Press
8500 Normandale Lake Blvd., Suite 180
Minneapolis MN 55437-3803
Phone: 952-820-0360
Fax: 952-893-0502
ISBN: 1-890965-07-3
For information on group purchase pricing call:
800-236-5885

Dedication

We dedicate this book to our clients for their willingness to accept our suggestions, and for sharing their remarkable success stories. They honor us with their "leap-of-faith" trust and they fill our hearts with their expressions of gratitude.

To our spouses, Dr. Wendy and David, who tolerated our endless hours of collaboration and lost "play time"—we look forward to making up for this.

To our readers, who deserve nothing but abundance and ease as they assist clients in profound ways. Sales is supposed to be an enlightened path to helping others, and not a slimy process of manipulation. Let this book help you enjoy it as such.

ABOUT THE AUTHORS

Roxanne Emmerich is the most in-demand *transformation agent* in financial services today due to her astonishing ability to create *profound change*. Repeatedly and predictably, she helps clients double, triple, and quadruple their growth rates within six months. *Hundreds of clients have doubled their customer satisfaction scores within 30 days of one session with her.*

Roxanne is the *CEO of The Emmerich Group*, whose client list includes the top-performing financial services firms in the country—and those that are wildly committed to being on that list. One of her previous books, *Profit-Growth Banking*, has been repeatedly referred to as the **"bible of successful banking."**

As a result of her record-breaking careers in both banking and brokerage, she was regularly asked to share her strategies with colleagues at industry conferences. Years later, *Sales and Marketing Management* magazine named her as *one of the twelve most requested speakers in the nation* for her ability to create immediate and profound transformation.

Her unique approach blends kick-butt marketing; enlightened, no-excuses leadership development; profit-rich sales strategies; and ironclad templates and systems. She presents this mixture to leaders, and then teaches them how to create "employees on fire." The result? **CEOs say, "It's a miracle."**

Roxanne is an owner and founder of two financial services holding companies, as well as several businesses. She has been recognized as *Entrepreneur of the Year* several times, and was singled out by the University of Wisconsin as the Distinguished Alumna of 2003.

For the past twenty years, Terry Slattery has helped clients grow their margins exponentially. He has trained thousands of companies to *increase their top-line revenue while decreasing their selling costs.* He has provided services to companies in more than 100 industries, from home-based enterprises to Fortune 100 companies.

He is the creator of "Wimp Junction," a program that *has taught thousands of sales people how to recognize and eliminate nonproductive sales behavior*, especially during complex sales.

Terry still holds *the record at IBM for opening the most accounts*—even though he hasn't worked there for twenty years. As a Sales Executive at Digital Equipment Corporation, he managed global relationships for the largest accounts, selling engineering systems, data communications, decision-support systems, and transaction processing.

When he is not helping companies grow, his interests include playing blues and jazz piano, as well as searching for the world's spiciest cuisine.

In *Profit-Rich Sales*, Roxanne and Terry share a sales system that is guaranteed to *turn your commercial lenders, trust officers, private bankers, and financial reps into weapons of "competitor destruction."*

OTHER TITLES BY ROXANNE EMMERICH

Profit-Growth Banking: How to Master 7 Breakthrough Strategies of Top-Performing Banks
Hardcover, 294 pages • ISBN 1-890965-04-9 • $29.95

*"Roxanne Emmerich strikes gold with this **must read** for all bankers. This book draws the map that can **create major stockholder value!**"*

-Jeff Schmid, President
American National Bank, Omaha, Nebraska

"This book is an outstanding source of wisdom and strategy for all bank leaders who want to grow their teams from 'order takers' to persuasive sales professionals... Roxanne Emmerich is the recognized expert in the field, and this book is a winner!"

-Nido Qubein, Chairman, Great Harvest Bread Co.;
director of an $83 billion financial institution;
founder of a community bank

Thank God It's Monday: How to Build a Motivating Workplace
Paperback, 44 pages • ISBN 1-890965-00-6 • $6.95

"Perfect! Finally, the toughest subjects presented with straightforward, common-sense solutions."

-Warren Chirhart, Customer Satisfaction Manager, 3-M

"Innovative, creative, yet practical. What a combination!"

-Jack Frick, Manager of Performance Development,
SECURA Insurance

TABLE OF CONTENTS

ACKNOWLEDGEMENTS

John Milton said, "A good book is the precious lifeblood of a master spirit." However, it was not the spirit of one that made Profit-Rich Sales a reality, but instead the collaboration among several ambitious minds who pulled together to create the book you are now reading.

It was just four months ago, in the spring of 2005, that the two of us decided to put down on paper what had become our passion—inspiring results. But passion alone was not nearly enough to produce a publishable book the first time around. In fact, the material needed to go through several stages before it was transformed into a book that could be of actual value to our readers.

From transcribing, to editing (and re-editing), to typesetting, to cover design, to reviewing, and then doing it all over again, there are many talented individuals to thank for getting the final version of ***Profit-Rich Sales*** ready for publication.

Much thanks to Cameo Publications for providing direction. To Dawn Josephson, for her numerous reviews to ensure our readers could understand and benefit from the material. To David Josephson, for his attentiveness in typesetting.

For the playful graphics that help readers make that final connection with the concepts, thank you to Lisa Irsfeld for creating the book's visual appeal. Your complete willingness to play around with our ideas made it easy on us. Thanks too to Mark Beaudry for his work on the eye-catching cover design. To Dave Denney for his exceptional photography.

Thanks to Laurie Gibson for her expertise on the final edits before print. You leaped over tall buildings in a single bound.

Thank you to the many trusted friends and experts in the financial field who reviewed the manuscript. Your valuable insight was key to finding the missing links in the material. In particular, we wish to thank Archie McDonnell Jr., David Barr, Chris Bart, Curt Hecker, Phil Koning, Lauch McKinnon, Mike Riley, Alan Rowe, Ben Smith, and Patti Steele, who contributed by reading and enhancing the book.

Many in our offices have been the drivers of Profit-Rich Sales. Involved at every step of the way—Judy Weiss, Rose Larsen, Larissa Williams, Abbey Karich, Lisa Engelmann, and Sarah McClain—it would have remained a heap of ideas with no outlet had it not been for all of you.

We are blessed to have been surrounded by people of extraordinary character and insight. And we are grateful.

INTRODUCTION

Have you ever experienced one or more of the following scenarios?

- You call a prospect for months, give her an infinitely better proposal than what she currently receives from the competitor, and after you have sweated and toiled over creating a powerful solution for her, she takes your ideas and implements them with a competitor who came in at a better price.

- You call on a potential client every year at renewal time to see if you can win the deal *this* year. Every year he meets with you, sucks you dry of all your beneficial insights and wisdom, tells you that you're close—but rewards your competitor with the business.

- A prospect tells you that you won the business. You "high five" everyone on your team. As you begin to implement, the client doesn't return your phone calls. Then "the call" comes: She is terribly sorry, but the incumbent, when told that they were being replaced with your services, said they could do all the same things—for less. You're out; they're in.

- You secure the deal, and the incumbent says they will undercut. The prospect then says you can keep the deal *if* you match the incumbent's pricing.

If you answered "yes" to any of these scenarios, you are not alone. The "sales slap" happens every day to those who don't know about the system that ensures you never get slapped again.

The sales slap is similar to training a dog. If a dog encounters a particularly vicious creature in the woods, he is reluctant to go back there again. Like the dog, you grow wary of "going back into the woods"—of giving answers, solutions, or quotes to certain prospects—but *unlike* the dog, you ignore your instinct and go back anyway. Why? For many years, when these prospects asked for a proposal, bid, or quotation, you worked long hours to provide the prospect with the best you had to offer, only to get rejected. Then two or three years later, the prospect comes back, asking you to do it all over. And so you invest hours of labor, only to be rejected again.

Then the epiphany occurs: You realize that a dog might be smarter than you are. Spot learned his lesson after only one unproductive experience. You, on the other hand, keep going back, using a sales process known as "Propose Everything You've Got, Cross Your Fingers, and Wait."

This "wimp party" is one of the major problems in today's financial services sector. To solve this, you must first understand it. In this case, what is the problem? The fact that the prospect falsely promises you the business only if you first *show* them how well you can solve their problems? The fact that the prospect found a better deal? No. Neither of these is the *real problem*. The real problem is that you don't realize how your customers and prospects draw you into this expensive and time-consuming competition, a competition that holds a very uncertain and often heartbreaking outcome. Because you don't understand this, you "wimp out" and allow the prospect to draw you back into their cycle again and again! However, once you recognize and understand this problem, you can immediately break through to more sales at higher profit margins.

In order to understand how prospects draw you into giving away all your secrets while not paying you, you have to figure out how they enticed you in the first place. Prospects have a system—a four-step system they use consistently and effectively to make you "give away the farm."

Here's how it works:

Step 1: The prospect lies to you (cynical, but true).

> Yes. Prospects lie, not necessarily because they're bad people, but because it's a way to get you to offer your ideas, solutions, and best prices without making a commitment to pay for them. Somewhere in "prospect school" they learned that lies to salespeople don't count. The prospect ropes you in like this: They tell you they're *not happy* with their current financial institution and that they're open to *considering a change*. Therefore, they'd like you to show them what you have to offer. Sounds reasonable, right?

> Of course this works on you because you have been trained to believe that salespeople should be optimistic, aggressive, and hard to kill—that you should give and give and give, no matter what, to get the business.

Step 2: The prospect gets your ideas, expertise, and quote— *but you don't get paid.*

> You show them how to turn their life into bliss—you

17

present a proposal, bid, or quote for what you would provide and charge to create this paradise. This requires that you put together all of your best ideas, solutions, and prices. You think this will surely get you the business.

This step is very time consuming and expensive. But it's worth it, right? They've just told you that they *really* like you, from what you've heard so far, you're practically a shoe-in.

Step 3: The prospect lies again—The "Think it Over" Lie

After you have showed them how you would solve all of their financial problems, your prospect will tell you, "You've really given us a lot to think about. This looks good. We'll get back to you as soon as we've had a chance to think it over. And by the way, you won the award for the best-looking proposal; the receptionist has a small trophy you can pick up on your way out." You leave actually feeling good, until you figure out what is happening!

Step 4: The prospect ignores you

The prospect has told you, "It looks good." You put the business on your 100% forecast. It's a sure deal. Your solutions were clearly the best. You call to follow up, and call to follow up, and call to follow up. You leave voicemail messages and send e-mails. At this point, only one person on the planet doesn't realize this opportunity has concluded—you!

You didn't have to be in sales more than a couple of weeks to realize that the prospects took the information you gave them in Step 2 and went shopping. They educated your competitors and the incumbent with *your* best ideas. And then, to add insult to injury, the incumbent competitor responds with a plausible offer that causes the prospect to implement much of *your solution* without having to go through the pain of changing business relationships.

You have just provided a valuable service to your prospect—***unpaid consulting!*** And a consultant who doesn't bother to get paid tends to have a short, stressful business career, and raises very skinny children.

At this point, you're tempted to say, "Gosh, maybe I should have discounted?" But think again.

The Doom of Discounting

We've heard it time after time after time. A salesperson says, "Sure, I can get the deal if I match the price."

Although that may be true, matching the price is something that doesn't require a salesperson—it can be accomplished over the Internet.

Many top performers know the formula to command premium pricing and how to stand tall when charging more for their premium value; they outshine their competitors by consistently getting deals at extreme premiums. They laugh at those who believe that a deal has to be matched—because they know how to repeatedly overcome the price resistance.

The good news is that YOU can do the same—IF you know what they know and do what they do. Remember, the sales process is a system that, if followed meticulously, has quantifiable results.

First of all, you need to understand the Doom of Discounting:

THE DOOM OF DISCOUNTING

Normal % of profit on selling price	% price cut	% Increase in sales to make same dollar profit	Normal % of profit on selling price	% price cut	% Increase in sales to make same dollar profit
20%	5%	27%	**33.5%**	5%	12%
	10%	80%		10%	29%
	15%	240%		15%	55%
				20%	100%
				25%	200%
25%	5%	19%	**35%**	5%	11%
	10%	50%		10%	26%
	15%	113%		15%	49%
	20%	300%		20%	87%
				25%	163%
30%	5%	14%	**40%**	5%	9%
	10%	35%		10%	20%
	15%	70%		15%	36%
	20%	140%		20%	60%
	25%	350%		25%	100%

Before attempting to increase sales by discounting prices, do the math!

EXAMPLE

Sales $5,000
Margin of profit 25%
Gross profit 25% of $5,000 = $1,250
Proposed price cut 10%

New sales volume for $1,250 profit
$5,000 + 50% of $5,000 = $7,500

As you can see by this model, if you have a normal profit of 25% built into your business model and you discount 10%, you need a 50% increase in sales to make the same amount of profit. That's profound!

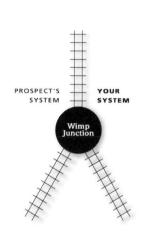

PROSPECT'S SYSTEM   YOUR SYSTEM

Wimp Junction

At this point, everything may be sounding all too familiar. Thousands of salespeople will assure you that they've seen the prospect's four-step system work. In fact, it's an excellent system, IF you're the prospect. But if you're the salesperson, it's a wretched waste of effort and time and has you heading for one big train wreck. You need to recognize when you reach "wimp junction"—the place where you have the choice to either wimp out and follow the prospect's system or follow your system—and learn to notice when you start using the prospect's sales system before it's too late. Keep in mind that, unless your boss wants you doing charity work between 8:00 a.m. to 5:00 p.m., discounting is NEVER the answer. The answer is following a system that assures that you have profit in every deal.

WHY DO WE LET THIS HAPPEN?

For years, "sales gurus" taught the age-old method that follows this sequence: qualify the prospect, propose a solution, and *try* to secure the sale.

The theory of this method is that you "build" off of the previous step—and if you have trouble closing, that means you did NOT, in fact, qualify the prospect AND/OR you did not successfully propose the solution. As a result, your spirits are low, and you have little faith in your sales ability.

The truth is that you *may not* be properly qualifying your prospects, and you *may* need work on your proposal—all of which you will learn here. But the real problem is that you are completing the process in the wrong order. To have a closure rate of at least 90%, **which you should have,** you must *qualify the prospect, secure the sale, and then propose your solution.*

QUALIFY   SECURE   PROPOSE

At this point, you're likely saying to yourself, "How can I possibly close a sale before the solution has been presented? It can't be done." Let us assure you: you *can* do it, and you will earn a lot of money in doing so. We know this process works because we've seen it transform results for over 20 years for more than 2,000 of our customers. And better yet, it works in all industries and all markets.

How many times have you given your presentation, and then wondered if you will get the deal? You've spilled all of your goodies on the table, crossed your fingers, and hoped the prospects liked what they heard and saw. You may have had a good feeling or a bad feeling, but you really didn't know what the future held. Realize *now* that you don't have to give up your "secrets" before you are assured the sale. And chances are, that is exactly what you have been doing if you're not closing 90% of your prospects.

You must avoid this fateful sales mistake and refuse to follow your old process—or worse yet, the prospect's process. Rather, take charge of your time and expertise with the Profit-Rich Sales System.

THERE IS A BETTER WAY!

Take your own track. The purpose of this book is to help you recognize when you approach "wimp junction" and how to get on the Profit-Rich Sales track. The Profit-Rich Sales System is designed to help you finally get higher yields, close in less time, obtain higher profit margins, and get rid of disappointing sales results once and for all.

Despite popular opinion, sales is just like any other type of business—accounting, engineering, or manufacturing—in which the discipline requires a proven process. Accountants can't successfully complete their end-of-the-month work without following a standard process. If they veer from the process, mistakes will surely surface before the year is up. Likewise, a manufacturer must develop a plan that pinpoints exactly what needs to be done and in what timeframe so that the product is shipped off and in stores on time.

Although all industries regularly use processes and systems, most people consider sales a "black art" that is not subject to control or predictability. This is because they have no selling process, so the art isn't understandable to them. They don't have a system.

So, what is meant by system?

A system must demonstrate two qualities:

- First, it must have defined steps that are clearly performed and, when executed correctly, provide expected results.
- Second, it must have a concrete method of measuring the progress made.

The system we are about to share with you may differ from what you are used to. You will learn how to gracefully lead the prospect through your process, ensuring that you don't waste your time, get pulled into a price war with a competitor, or get yanked back into parts of the prospect's sales process.

The Profit-Rich Sales System

If you are getting the "we'll think it over" response repeatedly, then you NEED Profit-Rich Selling, especially if you're closing ratio is less than 90%. The idea is to follow a sales system—YOURS. When you're not clear on YOUR system, you end up following your prospect's system, which means: working too hard for prospects you should have quickly disqualified, getting caught in the price war and having to match deals, and having closing ratios less than 90%. Many clients tell us their closing ratios move from 30% to over 90% by simply putting this system in place.

If you are going to use your time and expertise more effectively, you will need a process that is stronger and more robust than the one used by your prospects. The Profit-Rich Sales System is a sales process designed to counter the prospect-friendly "Propose the Solution and Try to Close the Sale" system.

Profit-Rich Sales:
7 Steps to a No-Fail Sales System

Consider what it would mean if your closing ratio was 90% on all sales presentations AND you were being consistently paid a premium over your competitors. What would it mean if you understood the rules of the game more completely so that you encountered fewer surprises and had more control over the sales cycle? We've been told thousands of times it is well worth the effort.

You have probably noticed that the "old school" sales approach often puts you in an uncomfortable position—either "pushy" or "pathetic." But our new approach puts you clearly in the position of being a professional who is committed to helping the prospect in profound ways—a far better position. IF IT FEELS LIKE SALES, YOU'RE DOING SOMETHING WRONG!

Challenge yourself throughout this book. Continually assess, redesign, and implement what you learn. For free action plans and templates to help make implementing easier, visit www.EmmerichFinancial.com.

You might not agree with some of the concepts we share. Many items might even make you feel down right uncomfortable, but do yourself a huge favor and try this sales process; one that has been found to be a profoundly better way to approach sales. If you don't achieve the results you desire, which is highly unlikely, you can always go back to your old ways of presenting to unqualified prospects and losing deals to competitors.

Trust us when we say, the results will follow just as they have for others before you. Enjoy the journey!

STEP 1 OF PROFIT-RICH SALES:
PROCESS AGREEMENT

ROAD-TO-RICHES GROUND RULES:
HOW TO STOP BEING A WIMP

T ime and time again, you give potential clients an offer, and instead of moving right along to the close, your prospect wants to "think it over." Sound familiar? This is a sign that you have probably presented too soon. The "think it over" response is a direct result of the all-too-common *premature presentation.*

To avoid the "think it over" response, agree with the prospect from the start about the communication process the two of you will use from that point forward. This type of process agreement ensures that *you always have a real (not fluffy) commitment regarding the next step.*

Why do you need a process agreement?

When you create a clear communication process, you also set expectations for the relationship. A process agreement:

- Establishes roles and goals for meetings.
- Creates comfort and acceptance for an early "No." If you're go-ing to get a "No," you want it as early as possible so you can

move on and use your time productively with other qualified prospects.

- Ensures that the meeting outcomes are addressed and agreed upon early in the sales process so you don't have numerous meetings that end with an inevitable but never-discussed outcome.

- Guarantees adequate time for the initial call/meeting.

- Sets the stage for more open and honest communication. Any psychologist will tell you that you *teach* people how to treat you. If you approach the prospect as a sniveling, begging, or aggressive salesperson, you will be treated like one. But if you position yourself as a legitimate, successful resource with limited time and a tremendous ability to solve problems in that time, you will be treated as such.

Establish early on the amount of time available for discussions, as well as the mutual outcomes you both are seeking. Then, you can *both* decide whether or not to proceed.

By doing this, you begin to ***train your prospects***. They will know that when they meet with you or *anyone* from your organization, there will be open, honest, and clear communication that will result in specific outcomes.

Remember, your company will not go out of business if you don't get a specific account. You have to close somebody, but not *everybody*, and you must accept the fact that the prospect may or may not become your client. Nonetheless, you avoid the "think it over" option. At this point, the only determination is whether the two of you fit so that you have a connection that will allow you to proceed to the next stage of the sale.

Be Positively Negative

Let's face facts. When ambitious salespeople do a song and dance, telling the prospect why they're great and showing signs of invincibility, the prospect has no choice but to put up their defenses to prevent being overwhelmed. Although these types of salespeople are charming and get points for enthusiasm, prospects respond to this situation by becoming more guarded—and less likely to buy.

When Terry's daughter was a high school sophomore, he noticed on the calendar that the spring prom was coming up. He also noticed that a pad of paper divided into two columns sat beside the phone. The left column listed the young men she *wanted* to invite her to the prom. The right column listed those boys who had *already* expressed interest in taking her.

Which column do you think interested his daughter the most?

If you guessed the left column—you got it!

The unavailability of the *potential* prom dates made the left column most attractive. Sure enough, as soon as a potential prom date moved from the left column to the right, Terry's daughter was not nearly as interested in the boy—she wanted to see who else was out there.

The same phenomenon occurs in sales. The story of Terry's daughter demonstrates a point of human nature you can use with all prospects: People tend to be most interested in things that may not be available to them. When you take this position early, not only are you approaching them in a way that's completely different than the last salesperson, but you're creating an atmosphere where both of you feel at ease to say "no" if it really isn't the right fit. Imagine the time and money you can save!

When a prospect "goes negative," so do you.

When prospects show signs of being negative about doing business with you, you need to be equally negative about the likelihood of your doing business with them. This doesn't mean you should insult a prospect. But try to refrain from being *overly* positive about doing business together in the future.

When do you go negative and what do you go negative about?

There are two times to go negative: when starting a conversation or a topic, and when responding to a prospect's negative comment.

1) Always start negative. It gives you more control because it forces prospects to sell to you—they need you to play. Until the prospect has told you they have a reason to switch to your company, there is *little* likelihood that they intend to switch to you, so build rapport by "going negative." You're no doubt wondering how a salesperson can be negative. But, that's exactly it. Most salespeople are overly positive, trying to convince their way into the prospect's wallet. Here's where you're different: You hold back. Remember, you want to remain on the left side of the "prom list."

Prospects will usually react negatively to a salesperson's same old "pitch." By beginning the conversation with some form of a negative comment, such as, "I don't know if we'll be able to help you," you can match this anticipated attitude. You have now caught the prospect off guard and established a level playing field, where you can move forward. This will prove especially helpful when you begin to establish the process agreement.

2) When the prospect gives you a negative response, you also respond negatively. If she says, "I'm happy with my current financial services institution," you could say, "Sounds like I'm here too late. Just out of curiosity, since no relationship is perfect, what one thing do you wish your current financial services institution did that they're not currently doing?"

If he says, "I don't have the budget to change to your organization's services right now," you can say, "Sounds like a problem. What would you like me to do?" What are you negative about here? You are only negative about the likelihood that you will be able to do anything to solve his budget problem. Nothing negative is being stated about the prospect, his company, or the competition.

Being negative allows you to meet your prospects where they are. You'll be in a powerful position, using a far more sophisticated technique than simply mirroring their behavior (e.g., crossing your arms when they cross theirs). Going negative frequently results in the prospect telling you why you should do business with him or her. There's nothing more convincing to prospects than hearing themselves explain why they should do business with you. Try it.

Notice that you're not pushing the sale. You're actually pulling back. Remember that potentially unavailable prom date? By starting out with this initial negative response and reacting similarly from that point on, you increase control in the new relationship and appear more interesting than your competitors.

Never be negative about the actual prospect or his or her current relationship with the competition. Instead, be negative about the likelihood of doing business. After all, you may find out that this actually is not a good fit. You might discover that you're too expensive or too big for what they want. This may not work for a number of reasons; be prepared by finding those reasons. This agreed-upon communication process and slight negativity will create more sales and will strengthen relationships with ongoing clients.

Remember, during the process agreement step, you and the prospect are agreeing to determine whether or not you bring value to the business relationship, based on a brief interview about the prospect's needs. If the answer is "no," you'll pack your bag and go home. If it's "yes," you will continue the conversation. Both prospects and existing clients will have the opportunity to find out whether or not you can benefit them, allowing for a professional relationship where both parties are treated as equals.

Use the following steps to establish a process agreement:

- **Step 1: Open with a subtle negative comment**
  - "I'm not sure we have a fit."
  - "We're not right for everyone."
  - "I don't know if I can help you."
  - "There is a lot to tell. I'm not sure where to start."

- **Step 2: Get permission to ask questions**
  - "Do you mind if I ask you some questions about your [challenge]?"
  - "Does it make sense if we ask each other some questions so we can figure out if there's reason to talk further?"
  - "I will need to ask you several questions. Will that be okay? I'm sure you will have some questions too, and I want you to feel free to ask me anything you want to know."

- **Step 3: Mention possible outcomes**

  - "At the end, we can decide if it makes sense to continue—and it may not."

  - "When we're finished today, we may want to continue, or we may decide there is no reason to."

  - "When we're done here, I'll tell you what I think makes sense, and you can tell me if you are comfortable with it."

  - "When our time is up, we'll decide what you would be comfortable doing as a next step."

- **Step 4: End with a question**

  - "Does that seem comfortable?"

  - "Does that make sense?"

  - "Are you okay with that plan?"

  - "Will that work for you?"

- **Step 5: Pose an agenda question about what to do next**

  - "We discussed (   ) on the phone, and that prompted you to meet with me. Are you still interested in that?"

  - "What would you like to accomplish in our discussion?"

  - "What were you hoping we could cover?"

  - "Would it be okay if I describe some of the problems we solve, and then you tell me if you want to know more?"

  - "I can tell you about (_____), or you could tell me what you'd most like to change."

  - "How would you like to start?"

Example:

"I appreciate your time today. I'm not sure if what we do is right for you, but we're going to know really soon.

Here is what I would like to do. Would it be all right if I ask you a few questions to see if the things we do that have helped other businesses would be of benefit or value to you?"

Note: It is important to let them know that your services have been proven to work well and that they are not acting as the test site.

"Obviously, you'll need to ask me questions about whatever you would like to know. We can find out if it makes sense for us to spend any more time together. That will probably use up the hour we have set aside. At the end of the hour, we will make a decision about whether we should see each other again, or if I should pack up and leave. Does that work for you? How would you like to begin?"

You are seeking mutual **agreement**. Notice that you didn't start with what you have to offer or how much you can help. You are *not* looking for an opportunity to submit a proposal. Instead, you start by simply agreeing on how the communication will continue between you and the prospect.

This ensures that you and the prospect are on the same side—you *both decided* to continue talking together—or to call it quits. The prospect's participation in this process allows for a much more open and truthful conversation. Your prospect will never be surprised about where you are leading them.

Everyone knows that there are "good" surprises and "bad" surprises. To eliminate the "bad" surprises from popping up on your sales radar, it's important to know where you're at with your prospect during every stage of your sales process.

Prospect Sifting:
Quickly Disqualifying Time Wasters

One of the surest ways to lose more high-profit-margin business is to work with unmotivated prospects. An obvious statement, yes? Yes. But this concept isn't always put into practice. Many salespeople spend inordinate amounts of time believing and hoping that their prospects either *are* or *will become* motivated. But if you want to follow a proven sales process, then you must *not* spend time with those who aren't motivated, instead spending *all* your time with those who are. Know the attributes of qualified prospects—and learn to spot them quickly. Here are some ways to determine if a prospect is truly qualified:

- **Your prospects tell you—in their own words—their reasons to change** business relationships or behavior. They are *ready* to make changes.

- **You have discussed the cost of their pain,** including all the ways they pay because they are not using your solutions. They agree that they *pay too much*, and don't want to continue what they're currently doing.

- **They are willing to spend more for the higher value you provide.** Their available budget to pay for your higher value has been discussed and agreed upon.

- **You understand their evaluation and decision-making process** regarding vendor selection. You can determine whether they will do business with you, as well as how they will choose from the competitors.

- **You have a commitment from them.** You know both *what* their decision will be (should you make an offer) and *when* they want the official relationship to begin.

You MUST investigate these elements thoroughly before you divulge anything about your products or services.

If you don't get any of these five signals from your prospective client, chances are you will do a lot of work—but not get the deal.

If you do an analysis of the business you've lost in the past, or the business you kept after you had succumbed to modeling a competitor, you can be *sure* that you skipped one or more of these five steps that reveal the five areas listed above.

The Profit-Rich Sales System leads you through this sales process step-by-step, so that by the time you put together your final presentation, you know you have a deal with acceptable profit margins. **You will maximize sales** *by following the simple rules outlined in the next few chapters.*

FAST-TRACK SITUATIONAL AWARENESS:

DISCERNING THE REALITY OF YOUR POSITION

One of the most valuable lessons learned in the military is the importance of maintaining "situational awareness": how much a person's perception of the current environment accurately mirrors reality. Quite simply, it's knowing what's going on around you. This awareness helps you to know where you are, what you should expect next, and what your course of action will be, depending on what happens. In the military, failure to maintain situational awareness could endanger your mission and ultimately your life.

While the sales team's success may not be as crucial as the military's, you can and *should* carry the same expectations. When you are finishing the initial sales call, make sure you are privy to *all* information. Know where the conversation went so that both you and your prospect know what the next step will be.

The easiest way to do that is to debrief yourself at the end of the call. It takes only a few minutes—and it does wonders for your sales efficiency. Establish what you achieved during the call so you can place it in one of the following four categories:

MUTUAL "NO"

Many calls will end in a mutual "no." This means you and the prospect have decided the relationship isn't going anywhere, and it makes no sense to continue.

MUTUAL "YES"

Some sales calls end with a mutual "yes." You and the prospect both agree that it made sense to continue the discussion. Then it's time to move to the next step in the sales process.

TIME TRAP

Some calls end in a time trap. These usually involve some sort of external future event, such as a board meeting that has to take place before a decision can be reached. Understand that a time trap is not a "think it over" or a stall, because you and the prospect have *agreed on exactly what happens* after you are released from the time trap. You have a clear, mutual agreement on what happens if the board votes "yes," or if it votes "no." You stay in control of your own selling process when you establish clarity about what happens after the time expires.

If you didn't get one of the three outcomes listed above, then you get the fourth, more expansive outcome.

CONTINUED PROFESSIONAL EDUCATION

The fourth outcome ends with your receiving some Continuing Professional Education (CPE). In other words...a lesson. The CPE outcome happens when you don't receive a mutual "no," a mutual "yes," or a time trap. When you realize that you didn't get one of the first three outcomes, review the call to determine where you lost control of the process. If you're a good student, the lessons you learn from this outcome can help increase your chances of success with future prospects.

Post-call debriefs are critical—and valuable. Remember, after each initial call, know exactly whether you have a:

Mutual "no"

Mutual "yes"

Time trap, with an explicit understanding of what happens after

CPE

Any of the first three outcomes is fine. The fourth outcome is less desirable, but can provide valuable learning (and you will eventually see less and less of it). ***Know which category accurately represents each prospect*** or you will waste precious time, annoy your prospect, and most likely, follow *their* sales process instead of *yours*.

We can learn some powerful techniques by looking at how professional athletes stay at the top of their game. After every play, an athlete analyzes his position on the field, examines the condition of the other team, and evaluates the effects of the latest moves—allowing him to best plan out his next actions. A successful athlete learns to do this automatically; it becomes a high-performance habit.

Remember, situational awareness means also knowing what went *right* (professional athletes review *all* their plays). What questions worked? Use them again so you can start selling smarter.

Your path to better results as a sales professional includes analyzing each sales call.

Beyond Logic:

Getting to the Take-it-to-the-Bank Emotional Buyer

No two prospects act the same when deciding whether to buy; however, most will fit nicely into one of two categories—the Logical Buyer or the Emotional Buyer—based on the way they make decisions. Here's how they differ:

THE LOGICAL BUYER:

- Is easy to find

- Is hard to close

- Has a limited scope of authority

- Is price sensitive

- Has a vested interest in not changing

- May bear the pain of change

- Thinks he or she is isolated from the consequences of not making a decision

When Logical Buyers talk to you, their motives sound like:

- "We are interested in…"

- "I am gathering information on…"

- "I thought we might like to have…"

- "We're investigating alternatives for…"

THE EMOTIONAL BUYER:

- Does not care about your "stuff"—your features and benefits, brochures, stories of great service, or tenured staff

- Cares deeply about the *consequences* of **not having** your solution, because one of the consequences is pain

- Experiences the financial burden of not doing business with you

- Is not price sensitive

- Can tell the Logical Buyer what to do because the Emotional Buyer gets the bill for not doing it—they are the ones paying, and they have the most votes in the economic democracy

When Emotional Buyers talk to you, their motives sound like:

- "We're unhappy with…"

- "We're disappointed because…"

- "We are frustrated regarding…"

- "I am fed up with…"

- "We are tired of …"

- "I am angry with…"

It's much easier to win a sale through the Emotional Buyer. Much more difficult is turning the Logical Buyer into an Emotional Buyer by telling them about the Emotional Buyer's pain; this may occasionally work—but not all the time.

To understand how to appeal to each of your prospects, you need to understand how they buy.

The Logical Buyer tends to be a technical person. ***Price is always their primary concern*** because the only way they can look like heroes is to beat you down on price, as opposed to working with you to create the best solution.

The Emotional Buyer makes decisions based on feelings and *then* builds the logic and justification for that decision. They feel the pain and often have to foot the bill for not fixing the pain.

Too many salespeople spend their time chasing Logical Buyers. By prospecting too far down the food chain, they waste countless hours with people who can't understand why the extra twenty basis points in your pricing will save them $200,000 next year while costing them only $15,000 more. Because "Nerdly" is responsible for just one small part of the budget—the part on which the $15,000 has an impact—he will sacrifice the $185,000 gain and feel brilliant about the money he saved the company.

Note: "Nerdly" is the guy who claims to have all the decision-making power, yet his wife won't let him leave the house with anything bigger than a twenty-dollar bill.

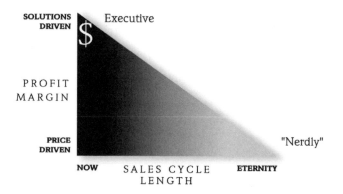

Meanwhile, Nerdly's boss, the CFO, searches frantically for a solution like yours, but doesn't even know you exist because the Nerdlies of the world forget to share this kind of information.

Here's an example of how this situation plays out in companies every day.

> Bob is in charge of purchasing at a large car manufacturing plant. He's found a brand of bolts that are 20 cents cheaper, shaving thousands of dollars from his budget. Now he can brag to the boss about how he is under budget by $50,000—and hopefully get that raise. Everything looks great for Bob, but Jane down in production is having some problems, too. The frames keep breaking, causing structural damage to the metal, and costing $1.5 million in repairs and production delays.

> The boss is glad that purchasing is under budget, but he can't understand why production is having so much trouble. The problem is that Bob doesn't see the consequences of using the cheaper bolts; Jane's the one who's feeling all the pain, as well as the boss—who's footing the bill. Jane wouldn't mind spending thirty more cents

each bolt for higher quality if it meant saving more than $1 million, and the boss, being the Emotional Buyer, would want that solution *now*. So if you're the bolt salesman, who would you want to talk with? You guessed it—the boss, the guy who pays the $1.5 million bill.

Below is an example of how this idea applies in the financial services arena.

Mike is an accountant at the plant headquarters and is in charge of choosing the financial institution the company will work with. He's found one that provides a scaled-down solution, charging $12,000 less than the other options available. The institution has set up its program for billing; the invoices go out the first and fifteenth of every month. Everything seems to be going well and Mike is eager to show how his choice has benefited the bottom line. However, all of Mike's "savings" are creating headaches in the customer service department. At around the first and fifteenth of every month, they are flooded with calls from customers who don't understand their billing statements. The customer service representatives spend days fixing billing errors and explaining how to read the statements, consuming precious time and resources. Customer service is feeling all the pain while the folks in accounting are feeling pretty good about saving a few bucks. The manager of both the customer service *and* accounting departments is the Emotional Buyer, someone who would gladly pay more to make all the calls stop, saving more than $800,000 each year in the additional staff-time now spent to handle all the calls. If she knew more about the approach and the institution her company is working with, the company would be doing something very different. Although Mike is the one making the decisions in this situation, you should actually be talking with the manager, because she's the one footing the bill for these "savings."

Simply stated, you need to sell to the emotional customer. Think about how a service or product you provide impacts your prospects. Who's most concerned about that impact, who feels the pain, and who foots the bill?

A big difference between low-performing and high-performing salespeople is that low-performers spend their time with the wrong people. If you're not talking to the person who suffers by not having your solution, you're wasting valuable time and assuring a low-profit-margin outcome, with you matching or beating a competitor's price.

Determine if your prospect is an Emotional Buyer or a Logical Buyer. If that person is an Emotional Buyer, great, but if not, move along and find a prospect who *is* an Emotional Buyer. Next we look in detail at a significant motivating factor in human behavior (which includes buying): pain.

Step 2 of Profit-Rich Sales:
Pain

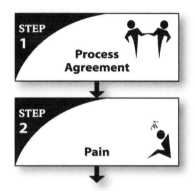

SALT IN THE WOUNDS:
HELPING PROSPECTS DECIDE QUICKLY

Consider this:

Rational people don't get up in the morning thinking, "Today is a good day to spend talking to a banker, insurance rep, financial rep, or trust officer." People have better things to do with their time.

The very fact that potential clients are either *taking your call* or *calling you* says they have something on their mind. Your job is to find out what that is—their pain. What pain would cause them to make a change? Knowing that reason will give you everything you need to complete the rest of the sales process.

If you don't uncover your prospect's pain, all you have is a prospect who is *intellectually curious* but not *economically serious*.

At this point, make it your goal to discover all the things your prospect would like to be different—or better—in their current financial business relationship. Uncover ways in which their current vendor serves them incorrectly and what they'd like to change. In other words, find the pain

51

they are experiencing. By asking pain-probing questions, you allow them to reveal the improvements they want. This also takes the pressure off you to talk in any depth about your pricing or about why they should consider your company.

Realize that when you approach prospects about a possible relationship, the prospect sees you as an *agent of change*. They know you want to talk them into changing their behavior. And what do we know about human beings and behavior change? **They hate it!**

The following questions illustrate resistance to change:

- How well do your prospects believe they are doing when you first approach them? The most likely answer is "Fairly well."

- How much fun is it for them to stop doing business with your competition and start doing business with you? The answer, of course, is "No fun whatsoever."

So why would they consider changing business relationships, and w*hat is going to cause them to do it?* This is exactly what you need to find out.

People will usually continue to do what they are currently doing until the consequences of that behavior become unacceptable. In other words: *painful*. Then, and only then, will they consider change.

Consider the following general principles...

- If the prospect feels there are no consequences to *not* being your customer, then you don't have a prospect. Rather, you have someone who has no intention of changing their current relationship. That doesn't mean they won't take your best price to their current financial services provider and use it to get a better deal.

That prospect will collect your information, shop you and compare rates, *but* will **never** become your customer.

- If people can refrain from becoming your customers and feel no consequences for doing so, then they have, in fact, made the *right* move.

- What about prospects who take an incredible amount of time to make up their minds? Prospects who endlessly delay, *thinking* that there is no cost associated with that delay. And if this is the case, they'll wait until they absolutely *have* to make a decision. Again, *you don't have a prospect*. In this situation—you have an opportunity to do unlimited, **unpaid** consulting!

People always move faster to deal with pain than to achieve pleasure. Your job is to get **them** to tell **you** how much it hurts and how much they want it to end—**not** for you to tell them how great their life could be with you. Use your time to help them uncover the consequences they've had to put up with in the past, are dealing with now, and *will* experience. Try for all three: past, present, and future.

If you can get them to realize and acknowledge that these consequences are unacceptable, your sales cycle can become much shorter. The greater the pain, the shorter the cycle. You can transform them from intellectually curious prospects who think they don't need you, to economically serious prospects who can't live without you. If you uncover the prospect's pain and how it's affecting their business, you don't have to match the price of the competitor who's actually causing the pain. Heighten your prospect's awareness of their pain. Pain and emotion go hand and hand—and both lead to more sales!

At this stage, all you need to do is uncover the prospect's reasons for considering change. The rest will come later. *You ask the diagnostic questions* and *they tell you* where it hurts. **The pain has to be in *their* words**. In this conversation, the prospect should be talking 80 percent of the time, and you should be asking and probing the other 20 percent.

This stage is crucial to the success of the sales process. Why? If prospects don't tell you about the pain they are experiencing and their reasons for wanting to change, then they aren't *your* prospects. Remember, you are the salesperson. Prospects sometimes think what you say might not be truthful. However, they believe that what comes out of *their* mouths is true. And you know the old cliché: The customer is always right!

If you don't uncover their pain, you may have a hope and a dream, but you don't have a prayer of getting their business. Don't position yourself so that others can bid against you—that's not your game!

6

NASTY FAT WORDS:

TRAPPING THOSE UGLY LITTLE WORDS PROSPECTS USE TO STRING YOU ALONG

> **fat word** (făt wŭrd), *n.* Statement a prospect makes that has more than one meaning. The salesperson has no way of knowing which meaning the prospect is intending.

If you had a dime for every time you heard veiled truths and fuzzy answers from your prospects, you'd be rich. Ambiguities that prospects often give us are **fat words**. They can sneak these words in at any stage of the sales process, but will most likely use them when you start questioning them about their pain. Take care to identify these words and refuse to accept them.

Fat words have double meaning and can lead to different conclusions between you and the prospect, depending on who's doing the interpreting. Remember that **your definition doesn't count**; the person with the money has the only opinion that counts. So, you need to force the prospect to clarify their meaning. Do this by asking questions.

Here's what fat words sound like:

> "I'd like to see your **best price**."

Does a prospect *ever* accept a "best price" as a reason to change? Do you shoot for a "best price" on your proposals? How many times have you been disappointed to learn that *their* "best price" and *your* "best price" didn't match?

At this point, you say:

> "I don't understand what you mean by 'best price.' Can you help me?"
>
> "What would your 'best price' look like?"

Make them tell you **exactly what they mean**. If the prospect uses a word or gives you an answer that could have more than one definition, it's a fat word—and it needs clarification.

Recognize the commonly used fat words below:

> "We're looking for the **best deal**."
>
> "I'm going to be making a decision **soon**."
>
> "We're **considering** a new financial service relationship."
>
> "We'll **think it over**."
>
> **"Probably..."**
>
> **"Maybe..."**
>
> **"Depends..."**
>
> **"If..."**

Fat words cloud the sales process because they create false expectations. The prospect dangles a prize, but you'll never get it unless you understand fully what meanings lay behind these ambiguous words.

Your mission, should you choose to accept it (that means "if you want to make any money"), is to meet every fat word with a "safe move." And the safest move in sales is always a simple three-word sentence.

"I don't understand."

Keep whittling away at the prospect's fat words until you completely understand if their "We'll think it over" means "It's going to a committee that will decide in two years," if it means you're up against another competitor, or if it means something else altogether. Perhaps your prospects are only holding on because they didn't like a certain part of your competitor's proposal. If you intend to win the deal, you must know sooner rather than later all of the details of the sale.

Whenever you hear a word that could have two or more meanings, simply say, "I don't understand," and then repeat that phrase until you get a clear answer. You must know the rules of the game in order to win.

Without clarifying the fat words, you cannot know if the prospect is stringing you along for a time-consuming, unproductive ride, or if that person is truly giving you the rules of the game. Again, you must know the rules of the game in order to win.

High-performing salespeople are intolerant of fat words and know how to put each fat word on trial. In contrast, low performers hear fat words, accept them as reality, and live in a state of delusion about making progress with their prospects.

Put fat words on a diet. Drill down each fat word to the point where you know exactly what it means. The next chapter provides more detail on the different ways to do this. Getting past these "fat word barriers" assures you're on the path to making a profit-rich sale.

PAIN PROBES:
KILLER QUESTIONS TO
HELP AMPLIFY THE PAIN

A s you now know, you need your prospects to tell you about their pain. But how do you get them to do that? Most salespeople take a big gulp of air before smothering the prospect with how good, fast, easy, reliable, inexpensive, and reputable their goods and services are. They spend the entire call touting what their company can do, but something's missing. These salespeople are clueless; they don't know what the prospect needs. This is not sales; this is prospect torture.

If you've spent the whole sales call bragging about how great your company is, you haven't addressed any of the needs generated by the prospect's pain. In fact, they may not even be aware of their own needs and wants. Why? Simple: They don't wake up every morning wondering how their financial institution could better serve them. They don't know how much they're losing by not being your customer.

To you, the solution is clear, and the prospect should be jumping at the chance to work with you. There is a problem, though. The prospect sees you as an interruption, someone trying to "sell" them stuff. As a result their first few answers to your questions probably won't be forthright. At this point, the prospect is more interested in getting you to leave so they can get back to work.

Move past this challenge within the first meeting. Ask a "powerful pain question" and then begin drilling it down—most prospects won't reveal true answers or genuine desires after just one or two questions. It's not until the third level of questioning that you get deep enough to reach the *first possibility* of actual truth about their pain. Generally speaking, this is the first level that actually allows for productive results. Surface drilling will not get the job done; you might need to go four, five, six, or more levels deep to get to the mother lode.

This bulk of chapter presents a review of the different levels of questions, some pain-probe tools used to locate and reveal the pain, and the catch-all sweeper question. These are necessary to successfully address the pain—and lead you to a strong sale.

First, you must understand the different levels of questions, and the uses for each level.

Level 1: Probe question

Level 2: "I don't understand" question

Level 3: "Tell me more" question

When you are asking your prospects questions, they will respond with different levels of ambiguity. Proceed through the three main levels (listed above) by progressively asking more direct questions. (Any higher levels of questioning are just more specific variations of Levels 2 and 3.) By doing this, you learn the truth and consequently, earn your money.

Three Levels

Your first pain-probing question at Level 1 will usually receive a vague, unquantifiable answer—a **FAT WORD.**

"We will **take a hard look at your proposal...**"

What exactly does "take a look at" mean? There's only one person who knows what this phrase really means, and that's the prospect. Remember, at every stage of the sales process your prospect will use fat words—these words always lead to a breakdown of communication if you don't respond to them effectively.

Your Level 2 question might solicit a slightly more defined answer, but it's still fuzzy. Level 3 offers the first possibility, but not a *guarantee*, of truth. Keep in mind, when you stray from *your* process and start following the prospect's, you might have to go through eight or nine levels to get an answer that leads you to any sort of a breakthrough. If you reach this point, it means you've let them get away with Level 1 answers to **all** of your questions. You have lost control of the call. Instead of making progress by asking follow-up questions that dig deeper, you have to repeat Levels 2 and 3 several times.

Again, use phrases like "I don't understand" or "My fault—I didn't ask this right" to get clarity from prospects. Always respond to fat words with some variation of one of these statements. Don't let up until you fully understand every necessary component needed for you to make the sale.

Prospects don't care about you until they realize how much they need you. And your job is *not* to tell prospects they need you. It's the prospects' job to *tell you.*

Example of a Level 11 Pain Probe to Get to the Truth:

> **You:** "How much impact does it have on the bottom line to not have your line of credit adjust up in the spring?"

> **Prospect:** "Quite a bit." **(FAT)**

> **You:** "I'm not asking this right. How much do you experience in lost revenue in one year?"

> **Prospect:** "Hard to say." **(FAT)**

> **You:** "I'm sorry. I'm not making this easy to quantify. Let me do a better job at asking this. When you didn't have a line of credit that adjusts for seasonal fluctuations, what happened? How much would you guess you could have done in extra revenue had you had a line that adjusts?"

> **Prospect:** "About $3 million."

> **You:** "And your profit margin had been about 20 percent. Any reason that would change?"

> **Prospect:** "No, that is the same."

> **You:** "So, let's see, 20 percent of $3 million. How much is that?"

> **Prospect:** "About $600,000."

> **You:** "Hmm. That may not be enough to bother you."

> **Prospect:** "That's real money."

> **You:** "Well, how much profit would you have to lose to switch financial institutions?"

Prospect: "I don't know." **(FAT)**

You: "I don't understand."

Prospect: "Well, I guess over $100,000 would make a huge difference."

You: "When would you want this money loss to stop?"

Prospect: "I haven't thought about it." **(FAT)**

You: "I don't understand."

Prospect: "Well, I guess I'd want to make it stop immediately." **(FAT)**

You: "Today?"

Prospect: "Yes, today."

As you can see, it may take lots of clarifying questions to get the prospect to think about their pain and to give you a truthful answer.

Tool Kit For Questioning

Doctors use instruments and questions to help uncover the actual causes of clients' pain—and so do high-performing salespeople. The pain-probe tools listed below will help you to uncover your prospects' pain in a discrete, unobtrusive manner.

Pain Probe Tool A: Third-Party Story Technique

This tool enables you to describe a sensitive situation that is probably happening to your prospect—the key is to describe the situation in a neutral way that does not make the prospect respond defensively. The following is a sample of what this might sound like.

1. Negative Opening (similar to what was described in the process agreement)

> Examples include:
>
> "I'm not sure there is a fit."
>
> "You may have already solved this problem."
>
> "We may not need to spend time on this."

2. Third-Party Story

Share a story or situation that directly relates to the prospect. You can get away with highlighting all the mistakes of the company in the story because that organization is not personal to your prospect. Use the story to get prospects to think about similar problems they may be experiencing.

> Examples include:
>
> "You may not have this problem, but…"
>
> "A lot of times when I am talking to people in your position, the thing that drives them the craziest is…."
>
> "The biggest complaint I have heard from others in the same situation is…"
>
> "You may not have this problem, but many of the clients who came to me complained that their past advisor did not have semi-annual meetings to assess current investments and look for adjustments to their portfolio based on changes in the

economy, client goals, and other things that would improve returns or lower risks."

The beauty of this approach is simple: it's hard to argue with a story.

3. Open-Ended Question

The purpose of the open-ended question is to get the prospect to relate any part of the story to their current situation, and to admit that it applies to them. It also ensures that you don't get a "yes" or "no" answer. Use "who," "what," "when," "where," or "how" questions; these will lead you in the right direction. Notice that "why?" is missing from the familiar sequence—and for good reason. It will put people on the defensive, and the prospect might respond with "Are you stupid?" or with an attitude that conveys the idea "You're calling me stupid!" Avoid these roadblocks by simply not asking "why?" questions.

The main instrument of the third-party story is obviously the story. Going negative at the start catches prospects' attention, while the open-ended questions relate the story's lessons back to the prospect.

Note: Do *NOT* build this question in front of the prospect. Instead, develop it during your pre-call planning based on your research and the challenges you anticipate with the prospect.

Pain-Probe Tool B: Forced-Choice Questions

These sets of questions also use the negative-style opening, but then proceed with your presenting two unfavorable, but opposing, consequences. This forces the prospect to choose which hurts more—A or B—and without knowing it, admitting a pain. Follow their admission with another open-ended question.

Example:

> "I'm never sure where to start. Some business owners want to talk about how to increase revenue by increasing their capital. Others want to maximize their earnings by managing cash flow more effectively. Where do you want to start?"

> Presenting two opposing, but equally negative concepts will get prospects to reveal their pain. Why? They don't have the option to mask their pain by using fat words.

Pain-Probe Tool C: Assumptive Questions

The assumptive question is a powerful tool that can be effectively used when you're challenging an incumbent. Simply find something your prospects would want—that you assume the incumbent isn't offering—and raise the emotional bar by pushing prospects into an uncomfortable zone.

> Here is what it sounds like:

> "When you and your CEO sit down with your lender each year to review opportunities to grow revenue based on an analysis of your industry peers, what have been some of the best ideas that have come out of those meetings?"

You assume that the meeting did, in fact, take place, and that your prospects received huge benefits. This is a two-for-one deal. First, they probably should have been doing this, and they aren't. Second, you have uncovered a pain: they don't know what opportunities they are missing, nor do they know what it has been costing them *not* to know.

Pain-Probe Tool D: Role Reversal

The purpose of role reversal is to position the prospect to tell you the feelings that person has associated with a fact or number. The role reversal is used *after* you've used one of the previous tools to assess the severity of the prospect's pain. Start with the same negative opening and then question them on a specific problem.

As they respond to the previous tools and lines of questioning, the perception of their pain begins to intensify. Now, start honing in on quantitative responses, like the previous example of a Level 11 pain probe.

As soon as the prospect gives you a number, minimize that number—and you'll get a strong response.

For example:

"I wouldn't want to assume that's a lot of money, and it's probably not."

You might have some trouble from the prospect on this, but the purpose of this statement is to get your prospect to tell you their feelings behind this number, and to define whether this number is considered large or nothing at all to their institution. Usually they cannot wait to correct you! Now, who is selling *whom* on the severity of their pain? You force a role reversal, and all you have to do then is ask how much worse it has to get before they need a reason to change. The prospect has just sold themselves.

Now that you have some tools to work with and an understanding of the different levels of questioning, you can begin to see what it takes to make a premium deal.

How many pains and how deep do you have to go to get your prospect to commit to fixing their problem?

Prospects' pain varies in intensity. A sore throat is not the same as a broken bone. While one injured or ill person can wait to see a doctor, another has to be rushed to the emergency room. Think of the degree of intensity of your prospect's pain (or absence of pain) along this scale:

> **No Pain > Aware of Pain > Concerned About Pain > Committed to Ending Pain**

With each new exploration into a possible pain, use the pain-probing questions and tools to help prospects realize truths. Escort them to **commitment** territory, where they must agree to find a solution—and where they see that the only way to ease their pain is through you.

> **Note:** *It will be hard to get a prospect to commit to buy with just one pain*, unless the cost of not fixing it is absolutely unbearable and/or there's a deadline.

Most of the time, you will need *at least three* pains for commitment. Once you find the truth to one pain at Level 3 (or a deeper level of questioning), move on to another pain. If you don't get a hit on the next one, keep moving along until you do. Pain Probes **A**, **B**, **C**, and **D** below must all be brought down to truths before asking the sweeper question that closes in on the commitment.

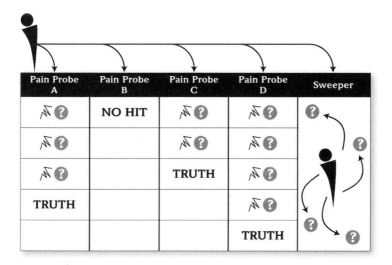

Pain Probe A	Pain Probe B	Pain Probe C	Pain Probe D	Sweeper
⚡❓	NO HIT	⚡❓	⚡❓	❓
⚡❓		⚡❓	⚡❓	❓
⚡❓		TRUTH	⚡❓	
TRUTH			⚡❓	
			TRUTH	❓

After hitting truths on **A**, **C**, and **D**, the prospect should have enough pain to become **committed to ending it**. Finish with the sweeper question.

Make a Clean Sweep

After you have hit three or more truths, the question below "sweeps" a broad stroke over all other areas by ensuring the prospect's emotional involvement. It serves a wide range of purposes by making sure you have not missed anything.

Your sweeper is very simple and will sound something like this:

"What else should we be talking about?"

"What should I have been bringing up that you would like to see different or better in your financial service relationships?"

Your killer pain probes have surely led you to a qualified prospect who is now fully identifying with the pain. However, you can also use the sweeper question as a last resort when all else has failed. Listen carefully to the prospect's answer—this may be a huge hot button for them.

> "Before we move on, what else were you hoping I'd bring
> up, and where would you like some more help?"

If they have a hurt, respond with:

> "I'll make a note of that, and we'll come back to it."

Prospects usually won't tolerate more than three or four pain probes followed by a sweeper question before they either ask you to prematurely jump to the presentation or they end the conversation. If you have this type of pain probe and sweeper process prepared before the call, you will be far more effective at getting the initial appointment—and the final sale. But there will be times when you've had a well-prepared call, used all the pain probes and a sweeper question, but still didn't uncover anything. In this situation, tell yourself that this is *not* a prospect, and move on. There is nothing you can do to help them.

Below is an extensive list of probes you can easily modify to fit your needs. Obviously, you can't use all the questions in one call. Select questions based on what you know of the prospect's industry or what you know about their business. The useful one will have the greatest relevance to the case you are trying to build, and will highlight your unique strengths (these are the basis for the USPs you will develop in later chapters).

Credit Probes:

- How do you currently use credit in your business?
- What changes would you make in your current credit relationship to help you achieve your goals more quickly?

- What are the constraints in your current credit relationship?

- How do they prevent you from achieving your goals?

- What do you like most about your current credit facility?

- Tell me one or two things you would like to change.

- When you told your current financial services professional about your plans to grow, what help did that person offer?

- When your current financial services professional has their quarterly meeting with you to help you grow, what have been the major benefits to your business from those sessions?

Private Client Services Probes:

- What strategies has your current investment advisor suggested to minimize your estate tax situation?

- What steps has your current trust officer taken to minimize taxes and maximize after-tax return?

- Who do you plan on giving your money to: the IRS, your kids, or someone else?

- When you did the business transition package with your attorneys, tax advisors, or financial services professionals, what was the result?

- When you have the monthly review with your investment advisor, what have been the most helpful outcomes of those meetings?

Employee Benefit Probes:

- How effective has your current EB package been in attracting and retaining employees?

- Tell me about your personal satisfaction with your retirement program.

- We've seen other business owners struggle with their personal retirement. How comfortable are you that you're going to reach your goals?

- How happy are your employees with:

  Returns on their investments?

  Reports they get?

  Response of help lines?

- Sometimes when I talk with business owners like you, they speak of their frustration that, after all the years and work, there is still a gap between what they hoped or needed their retirement fund to be and where it actually is. How are you doing in that area?

Treasury Management Probes:

These questions may be used for background purposes and may be asked of people at a lower level than decision-maker.

- Tell us what you like most about your current cash collection and disbursement process.

- What would you like to see done differently or better?

- When you asked your current financial services institution to reduce the delay in ([...]), what steps did they take?

- What has been the impact of your current cash management practices and reporting systems on your cost of borrowing?

- How much time and money are you spending for treasury management?

- How much time does it take your financial services provider to respond when a [unique opportunity] has presented itself and you need a quick credit decision?

- How much time does it take your financial services provider to respond when a check is canceled?

- Which of your current treasury services do you deem most important?

- How much time do your people spend reconciling, and what do you think is the cost of that time and effort to your company?

- When you need an answer from your financial services provider on cash position and it needs to be accurate, how long does it take to get it?

- The last time your financial services professional reviewed your treasury services, what were the benefits/changes/conclusions you felt were of greatest value?

- If you could change one thing about your current treasury services, what would it be?

You've probably already thought of many of these pain-probing questions, but have never asked them of prospects or clients because they seem rude. Or perhaps you think it's none of your business. The fact is that these questions are not rude, and if you want to get the deal, it is *your business*. Simply put: You will close more deals with higher profit margins if you get prospects to consider their pain and unmet needs. You choose the level of your success, remembering that greater efforts usually result in greater rewards.

FLIPPING STALLS AND OBJECTIONS:

HOW TO STOP THEM BEFORE THEY BECOME DEAL BREAKERS

A fter years of observing hundreds of sales calls, we've learned how to recognize a prospect's behavioral pattern. As discussed in the chapter on pain probes, most prospects will respond to your first level of questioning with some form of a stall by using fat words. Recognize **what a "stall" is** and **how it is enforced** so you can bulldoze past it in conversation with your prospect.

People find it difficult to change their views because they are usually unaware of the alternatives. Not only that, but if they don't see any *reason* to think another way and everyone *around them* thinks that way, what would provoke them to change? So, they stall when confronted. *Unveil the consequences—in big, red, blinking lights—they will face if they hold on to that hindering view.* This ensures that they have no choice but to take the chance of changing. But be careful: your prospects need to feel that they've made the discovery, and not that they were told what to do.

Respond to any stall by suggesting the possible consequences of not looking at the situation from another point of view. "How big would the consequences and pain have to be before you become concerned? At what point would you want to know about the adverse effects?" Be ready for your prospect to use a library's worth of fat words in response.

Remember when everyone thought the world was flat?

Around 1492, the prevailing view was that the world was flat, and if you sailed far enough in any direction, you would either fall off or sail into eternity. You can imagine how hard it was for Christopher Columbus to convince the venture capitalists to fund his exploration. They didn't want to lose their ships! Every time Chris tried to explain to them that he was looking for a new route to India, they answered without much thought, "Chris, our advisors tell us the world is flat!"

They pronounced their view of the world, and, in doing so, indicated why they didn't want to provide the ships for his adventure. They were stalling.

So Chris, not getting anywhere with his fundraising, figured out a way to get past the "flat world stall"—and just in time for his meeting with the Queen. After his presentation, he awaited the Queen's response:

> Queen: "Chris, I have trusted advisors, and they are telling me the world is flat."

> Chris: "Your majesty, I understand that. However, let me ask you this. If it were to turn out that the world is not flat and instead round, and if, because of that, we can be the first to reap the benefits of whatever we find, would you like to know?"

We all know that Chris got the deal. Every stall is some version of this story. The prospect has a certain view of the world, and because of that they will either act, or not. Their flat worldview accounts for their reluctance to change. However, once you probe them with your questions, and share with them the consequences of holding on to such an outdated view, they most likely will begin to embrace change.

Recognize and Respond

Approximately 80 percent of prospects are not very skilled in dealing with salespeople. They have essentially five moves when fending you off, and they use these moves when you start or end your pain probing. The five most frequent prospect stalls (presented below) will work on an unprepared salesperson. Don't let yourself be one of them.

Five Common Stalls:

1. "I am happy with my current financial services."

2. "I don't have time to talk to you."

3. "We were with your company thirty years ago, and you dropped us; we therefore decided never to work with you again."

4. "Why would I want a different business relationship?"

5. "If you can beat what Financial Services Institution X is charging, you'll have my attention."

A friend of Terry's retired, having spent the bulk of his career as a pilot flying large cargo planes across the Pacific. He tells a story of one of his last trips, in which the airplane was fully loaded. The airport was under heavy construction, and as they were taxiing on the runway, something happened to the aircraft. Apparently, additional stress had been placed on the tires, and as his plane began its takeoff roll, one of the tires blew. Fortunately, he was able to successfully abort the takeoff.

> Terry asked him, "Don, what were you thinking about as this was all happening?"

> He said, "They don't pay me to think. When something like this happens, they pay me to execute what they've trained me to do and what they know already works. They don't want me getting creative."

What a great answer for those of us in sales! If you don't anticipate your prospect's negative reaction, and are instead forced to cope with it in real time, you won't handle it nearly as effectively as you would if you had given it some forethought—and had a set of instructions to follow.

Salespeople struggle with stalls because they haven't planned for what the prospect might say and how they will handle each response. The unprepared salesperson is both surprised and under pressure to *create* an acceptable reply. They rarely pull through.

Don't expect to create the perfect response on the spot. Instead, be prepared by simulating the scenario *before* you go on a call. Sit down and visualize yourself handling the call effectively and comfortably. With enough practice you'll soon be on autopilot, responding the same way—and the right way—automatically, every time. You'll feel less pressure, act and react with confidence, and gain control of the conversation.

Your practiced replies to any one of the prospect's stalls must have two components:

1. Recognition
2. Response

The two components work together, allowing you to communicate with the prospect more effectively.

The "recognition" comes first. It sets the stage for the "response" and keeps it from sounding abrasive or irritating. The recognition component is just a simple statement that lets the prospect know you are listening. When you add the "response" component, you retain control of the discussion, and you advance the agenda.

Below are examples of recognizing and responding for the five different stalls.

STALL 1:

> Prospect: "I am happy with my current financial services provider."

> Recognition: "I'm sure they appreciate your business."

Then comes the "response," or your answer to their stall.

> Response: "Since you are already happy, what would I need to bring to this discussion for it to be of interest to you?"

By ending with an open-ended question (who, what, when, where, or how), you place the obligation to continue on the prospect.

STALL 2:

> Prospect: "I don't have time to talk to you."
>
> **Recognition:** "Sounds like I could have picked a better time."
>
> **Response:** "What would you like me to do?"

You may say to yourself, "I can't say that," or "That's uncomfortable." But it's really pretty simple. All you're doing is acknowledging the bad timing and asking them to tell you what to do. There should be nothing uncomfortable about this. If you say the usual, "When is a better time for me to call?" you begin the same old "I'm just a salesperson—go ahead and kick me if you feel like it" syndrome.

Instead, you're saving time by asking the prospect for direction. You're cutting to the chase: Does the person want to talk or not? If the prospect is going to tell you to take a flying leap, wouldn't you rather know that now—and not later? This will save you time and effort on those future unreturned calls.

STALL 3:

> Prospect: "We were with your financial institution, but...."
>
> **Recognition:** "Sure sounds like we could have handled it better."
>
> **Response:** "How can we begin to recover?"

STALL 4:

Prospect: "Why would I want a different financial institution?"

Recognition: "That's a good question."

Response: "What would you like to see your current financial institution do better?"

STALL 5:

Prospect: "If you can beat what Financial Services Institution X is charging, you'll have my attention."

Recognition: "I'm sure they have you on the 'A' list."

Response: "What are you paying for...?"

Note: You just want to know what the competition is charging. You have no intention of charging less!

Do you remember playing musical chairs? You only had a certain number of chairs, and there could only be one child per chair at the end of the song. Well, the same rules apply here. There are only two chairs: the "okay chair" and the "not okay chair." You and the prospect can't sit in the same chair, so it's your job to make sure that, at the end of the song, the prospect is sitting in the "okay chair."

In the martial art of aikido, when a fighter is being attacked, the primary method to beat the competitor is to step to the side so the attacker uses all his energy to attack while the aikido fighter's energy is conserved. The attacker wastes energy while the aikido fighter simply fights smarter.

The "recognition and respond" approach is exactly that—a way for you to win by rolling with your prospect's stalls while keeping your hands firmly on the reins. This type of "call control" will help ensure that you properly identify a stall when it comes at you, and respond with an appropriate reply. You can also make sure your prospect sits in the **"okay chair,"** meaning they are **okay** with the topic of discussion, and they are **okay** to continue. By keeping the prospect in the "okay chair," you give the illusion that they are in control, just like the aikido attacker. In reality, however, you are comfortably positioned to continue the qualification process.

On any given day, more than half of the population is "not okay." They're stressed, angry, feeling insecure, tired, hungry, etc. People don't buy when they feel this way, so the best way to put the prospect in the "okay chair" is to always put *yourself* in the "not okay chair."

You can put yourself in the "not okay chair" by saying:

"Sounds like I'm too late."

"I'm not explaining this well."

"Maybe I misunderstood something."

"I could be off-target here."

"It's possible I'm not getting this right."

If your prospects feel like they've thoroughly described their reasons for not doing business with you, but what they've actually said was little more than was a bunch of sentences filled with fat words and excuses, then you have some choices:

A)   You could say, "Let me tell you why my solution is better." This is essentially equivalent to telling the prospect they're being stupid by staying with your competitor. It puts *you* in the "okay chair" and puts the prospect squarely in the "not okay chair." This is what you don't want.

B)   A better response is to put yourself in the "not okay chair" by saying, "I must have missed something. Help me understand this…" By jumping into the "not okay chair," you make it easy for the prospect to sit in the "okay chair."

Obviously, you don't want the prospect in the "not okay chair" for any length of time. By using these methods, you can be sure that every time the prospect tries to switch chairs, you sit them right back down where they belong.

UNIQUE SELLING PROPOSITION:

ASKING FOR AND GETTING PREMIUM PRICING

I f you walked into a Lexus dealership and told them you were interested in buying one of their cars, but would not pay the high price they were asking because you could get a Chevy for $20,000 less, the employees would look at you like you were goofy. It would be a ridiculous statement. There's no way to make a comparison between a Lexus and a Chevy!

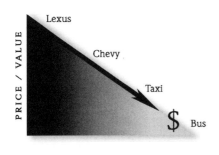

Yet, financial services professionals constantly take their Lexus-quality brand and get pulled into commodity pricing wars with Chevy-quality competitors. They sink to competing on price with their least mentally gifted and/or most desperate competitors. These Lexus-quality financial services professionals lose business they should have been able to obtain (or retain) at premium pricing.

Why does this happen? It happens because these financial services professionals have done nothing to differentiate themselves in clients' minds. As a result, they *have* to give Chevy pricing to prospects, even though they provide Lexus services.

This is where USPs, or Unique Selling Propositions, comes in—and *you need to have one—or more—of these.*

A USP is the definable difference that makes you worth more in the client's mind. The better your USP, the more you can charge. Therefore, you must invest considerable time and effort into creating your USP(s). Nothing pays bigger dividends.

What Sets You Apart?

Are you having trouble figuring out how to differentiate yourself because you think you sell commodities, and that all financial services institutions have the same products? Think again.

Now if you were selling vodka, then you might have a problem. Vodka is tasteless, odorless, and colorless. Vodka is the ultimate commodity. How do you differentiate that?

Some vodka companies tried to tout how the vodka was processed ("Triple distilled using only Russian rye.") while others explained the unique formula ("Made from a 100-year-old special recipe."). For years, vodka companies set themselves apart in this way, and it worked fairly well. Then a competitor came in with a powerhouse USP: "The only vodka that has a fruity taste *and* color."

Wait a minute. That's not fair! They reinvented the category!

How did it sell, you ask? Well, if you consider a **700 percent premium price** to be significant, then they did okay. By applying the USP rules, even vodka transcended the commodity image.

You can apply this principle to anything. If you wanted to buy jewelry, and you were on a block in New York City with ten jewelry stores, which one would you visit? If they all had only the owners' names on the front door, you would probably pick the closest one.

But, if one jewelry store owner put up a sign that read, "New York's Outstanding Jewelry Design Award-winner Four Years in a Row," you're not going to miss that one. If the store across the street had a sign that read, "The Largest Inventory of Unique 14 Karat Gold," you're probably going to stop there, too. Suddenly, the other eight stores on the block become invisible. And invisible is what *you* become when you don't have a USP that rocks.

How do you differentiate yourself so that you're able to charge premium prices? And then how do you sell that difference?

You must follow and apply the following rules (all three of them) for your USP to work. Don't make this hard—it isn't. This is not rocket science, and there is no one right answer. You should invent numerous USPs. Try out several to see which ones light up your clients' eyes.

THREE-STEP USP DEVELOPMENT FORMULA

Step 1: What do your customers want that they are not getting from your competitors?

> Do your competitors make an annual business call to give their personal financial advisors the chance to look for opportunities to make finances easier for their clients, including small business owners? Services such as

integrating Bill Pay with Quick Books or other software could be recommended. If your competitors don't provide this service, it then becomes an opportunity that's worth additional pricing! That could be one of your USPs.

If your competitor sends out a new lender to clients every six months, that "churn" impacts their clients. Your USP could be that your average lender is on every one of their accounts for over seven years. That means that clients don't have to waste time and money training a new lender several times each year. And that is worth premium pricing.

Make a list of all the things customers care about that your competition doesn't handle. Be specific. Don't make an ambiguous statement such as "customer service." Instead, define it with detail, saying, "The competitor doesn't go out to the commercial clients' businesses," or "They don't have a program where the client is continually working with a team of specialists assigned to their account." These "opportunities" could be the basis for creating a strong USP.

Step 2: Create a dramatic difference in the area of opportunity identified in Step 1.

If you don't have a dramatic difference, why not build it today? As they say at Nike, "Just do it."

For example, if clients want more of a relationship, and your competitors have an "open the account and then ignore the account holder" kind of approach, you could put in place a system so that you call all "A" clients quarterly to discuss how you can further help them. Additionally, you could hold semi-annual client seminars so they can learn new things about their finances, and you could send a series of "tips" or articles to clients via e- or regular mail. Having an actual system makes it much more believable and powerful than simply saying you are following up.

Similarly, if you hear complaints about your competitors from your special clients (the ones who used to be your competitor's clients), pay attention. Listen carefully when they say that their previous financial services institution didn't offer occasional reviews to cover new services like Bill Pay. (Note: not telling clients about new products is high on the list of complaints about the customer service of financial services institutions.) Create a semi-annual review process whereby you call every client and ask about their upcoming needs. You can then inform them of other services you offer, and ask if there is anything else you can do for them.

The point of this advice is simple: Zig where the competition is zagging poorly, and do it in a big way.

Then, after you have finished Steps 1 and 2, working them with a degree of success, it's time for the magic of Step 3.

Step 3: Define the USP as an explicit benefit explicitly stated.

You have undoubtedly heard the statistics about the number of marketing messages people receive each day—it's currently in the thousands. When you're competing with that much "noise," you have to make sure your message is not "fluffy." Explain the USP in detail, because the detail makes it believable.

Put yourself in the prospect's shoes. If someone is selling you car wax and says, "This is the longest-lasting wax," while the competitor across the street says, "This wax is guaranteed to hold its bead for six months," which would you choose? The one with the quantifiable results, of course!

Likewise, if you are buying ice cream, and the two shops next door to each other differ in only one area, you'll go to the one that differentiates itself from the other. To illustrate this simple idea, below are several ice cream shop USPs that show the power of integrating all three steps.

- *"Made from thick Jersey cream."*
- *"Over thirty-nine flavors in stock every day."*
- *"Frequent licker club: Buy five cones and the sixth one is free."*
- *"Voted by City Pages as the Best Ice Cream in Pleasant Town."*
- *"Over 98 percent of our customers come back with a friend."*
- *Make your own sundae. We scoop. You create."*

For these USPs, the ice cream shops can charge huge premiums. Why not? Starbucks did it with coffee—simply by differentiating itself.

If you tell prospects, "We really care about you," you'll be met with a "Yeah, right." But if you say, "We do things differently here. We don't want you to miss opportunities to maximize your returns and achieve your goals. To make sure we are maximizing your results, we have a yearly financial review by a personal financial services professional for all accounts with over $5,000 in cash, savings, or certificates." **Now you're talking their language.**

These are great approaches to USPs, and you can use *all* of them:

- **Explain your system**

  By telling prospects you have a Seven-Step-Mortgage Maximizer process, whereby you make sure they are getting the best mortgage for their needs (one that saves them the most money over the life of their mortgage), you suddenly are no longer competing against competitors who are simply quoting rates.

  By telling prospects you have a yearly review process, whereby the team assigned to their account will meet with them to find opportunities for them to efficiently grow their business, you'll surely sell several more services each year and bond the relationship, making it impenetrable.

- **Use statistics**

  "Ninety-six percent of our clients, when surveyed, said they would send a friend," is a much more powerful statement than "We have great service."

  You could mention the percentage of clients who stay with you each year, the percentage of clients actively using your Bill Pay service as opposed to the average in the financial services industry, the number of years of retention of accounts, what percent of the small business market you have, etc.

Be careful not to make ambiguous statements or say things that don't matter to the customer, such as, "We have over eighty-five years of combined experience." Who cares? That could mean you have eighty-five people who have all been there *one* year!

- **Reinvent a product**

   Just like the vodka company, you too can reinvent and position your commodity products in a new light. For example, why quote rates all day long on a thirty-year mortgage when you can have a "5 for 5" program, a five-year ARM that doesn't have the five fees buyers normally are charged elsewhere? You simply make up the fees in the loan pricing. In the process, you bring down the cost for many people who don't really need the rate to be guaranteed for thirty years. (They probably won't have that mortgage in five years, anyway.)

   Why not add unusual features to your current products, and rename? You could add sweeps from checking accounts to the savings accounts or mutual funds you offer and package it as a "Destined for College" savings account. You could create a special program for a parent with a child in college that sweeps an assigned amount each month to the student's account, with additional amounts swept for tuition at the beginning of each semester. The sky's the limit—your creativity will pay big dividends.

An example of a powerful USP was the Washington Mutual slogan, "It's not totally free checking if you have to pay to talk to a teller on the phone."

Wham! We're not sure which competitor they were slamming, but they hit some company where they were weak with a dramatically different message that both mattered to the customer and was defined in a detailed way.

How do you get started?

List your competitors' weaknesses. Then, for each weakness, create a dramatic difference between that weakness and your strength. Define that difference explicitly.

Keep doing this over and over again for each product—and for your entire company. Have a plethora of USPs. It will keep you out of the price war forever.

Your USP allows you to command premium pricing. Not having your USP should be costing the prospect in some way. Don't wimp out at this stage; the entire Profit-Rich Sales System depends on you commanding a premium for your differences.

For assistance and examples of how to develop powerful USPs specific to your needs, visit www.EmmerichFinancial.com.

FULLY-LOADED USP QUESTIONS:

MAKING YOUR IRON-CLAD CASE FOR PREMIUM PRICING

Once you have your Unique Selling Proposition, which clearly shows you have advantages that your competitors don't, make sure it passes the litmus test. It must:

1. Matter to the customer

2. Be dramatically different

3. Have an explicit benefit that speaks to the quantifiable results

Now you have a powerful way to prove to your prospect that you're worth more than the competition. You have no intention of matching the price of a competitor who isn't able to add the same benefits.

How you do that matters.

Your USP is the cornerstone of your pain-questioning process—it is what prompts the prospect to pay more for your difference. First, know how to word your USP question. The following two ways work best:

1. **Start with "How important is it to you to... (USP)?"**
Examples:

> "How important is it for you to work with a financial services institution that is open until 7 p.m. at least two nights each week so you don't have to take time off of work just to manage your money?"

> "How important is it for you to have a mortgage that doesn't have an origination fee or a closing fee?"

2. **Put your USP on steroids by using an alternative question pumped with two of your USPs.**
Example:

> "I'm never sure where to start. Many of our clients came to us because they were irritated that they had to do their financial business during work hours and it cost them lost time from their jobs. Others came to us because they were frustrated by having to pay excessive fees like origination fees and closing fees. Which of these is important to you—or is there something else you want to improve about how your financial services are handled?"

Whammo. Now, when your competitor is offering banking only during business hours, and has origination fees on *every* loan they offer, you have the prospect feeling very unsettled about that competitor.

When do you use the alternative USP question as opposed to the simple "How important is it for you to…." question?

The alternative USP question is a *great* opener.

Let's face it. Your prospect is not going to be inherently enthusiastic about changing relationships, as was previously mentioned. It takes work, time, and hassle to switch. Prospects will often live with mediocrity or even terrible service just to avoid the hassle of changing the relationship.

Now *you* come along. They *don't* see you as the savior. They see you as a threat. If they change relationships, it will involve some work.

Immediately win their hearts over by having them experience the pain of not switching. The alternative USP question is powerful for that.

Since your prospects aren't experiencing the benefit of your USPs, and they can clearly feel the pain of not having them, it is a double-barreled shot that helps them to see the light—that you are clearly a better choice.

Below are additional examples of those starter alternative USP questions:

> "I don't know if we're a good fit, but some of our clients who have come to us were frustrated by not having their personal financial advisor call them on a quarterly basis to uncover opportunities that would enhance their returns and save expenses. Others were frustrated because their brokerage accounts were separate from their banking accounts. This means they were receiving no help or guidance on integrating their financial services."

> "I don't know if we're going to be able to add value for you. Some of our clients tell us that they were frustrated by not having a financial services team that looks for the best way to structure the loan with the deposit accounts to maximize returns. Others end up coming to us because they wish their advisors would visit onsite occasionally

to help with things like integrating Bill Pay with their accounting system so they wouldn't have to waste hours doing additional unnecessary transactions."

Ouch! Suddenly you have prospects who are, at the very least, a little irritated at their current financial service provider. You'll want to ask questions that help your prospects clearly realize the pain they have as a result of not having the benefit of your USP.

STEP 3 OF PROFIT-RICH SALES:
ECONOMICS

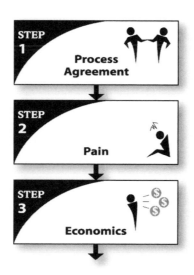

SHOW ME THE MONEY!:
STRAIGHT TALK TO PROFITABLE DEALS

A s previously discussed, when looking at the forces behind uncovering a prospect's pain, emotion determines almost every decision people make. But we also need to prove to ourselves that we are rational beings. Therefore, we want to be able to justify our emotional decisions with an iron-clad story of why it makes economic sense.

Additionally, when we want to document our rational case, it is far more powerful if we come up with the supporting case ourselves rather than someone dictating to us the reasons behind the decision that was made.

If you understand the following two principles: 1) emotional buying shored up with logical reasoning, and 2) the need to come up with one's own rational evidence, then you can help any person who has reasons to buy. That is, to buy *and* come up with the *budget* to buy.

What do you cover in the "economics" discussion stage?

- The cost of the problems you have uncovered
- The investment available for the solution
- The willingness to pay

If you don't have the money talk *before* you propose, you are guaranteed to meet price resistance and can potentially get pulled into a price war with a competitor. *Your profit margins will be skinny!*

When prospects get in touch with their pain, and they understand the economics of not doing business with you, they will have no problem with your fees.

Example:

> Let's use the same lender situation we discussed when developing your USP—taking it one step further this time.

> Your prospect's current financial services institution has had a new lender on their account every six months for the last three years. At this point, it sounds like an annoyance. Help the prospect logically reconstruct this *annoyance* into an economic *problem* that they would be insane not to fix. Conveniently, one of your USPs is that your lenders have all been with your company for at least seven years. You need to help your prospects put two and two together to see how it benefits them.

Let's take this through the process.

You: "When your lender changes every six months, what does that cost you in terms of lost time as you reeducate every new lender about your business?"

Prospect: "Well, I guess I spend an extra two hours of my time, and I'd value that at about $500."

You: "I'm not asking this right. (Always take the blame for not getting the answers you want. **Never tell them they're wrong**.) Besides the opportunity cost of your hours spent retraining, if you were to estimate—and I know it's a guess—but if you were to estimate the cost of not having your lender know your trends, seasonal adjustments, customers, opportunities, and threats, what do you suppose the fact that your lender can't spot opportunities for you to grow your revenue or decrease your expenses costs you?"

Prospect: "Gee, I don't know." **(FAT)**

You: "Yes, I'm sure it's impossible to know—but what is your guess as to your lost revenue?"

Prospect: "Well, we didn't have enough inventory in November because our line didn't adjust, so that probably cost us anywhere between $75,000 and $100,000 in lost sales this year."

You: "And usually when you lose sales in one year, there is an impact: some of your customers became someone else's customers, so there is a recurring yearly impact. What would you guess that would be?"

Prospect: "Well, at least $50,000 each year."

You: "And if that continued, how much new damage and how much recurring damage would happen each year?"

Prospect: "I guess that number would be an additional $50,000, so that would grow exponentially. I guess after five years, it's going to cost me at least a quarter of a million to a half of a million dollars."

You: "How about the cost of not reducing expenses through the recommendations that an organization like ours makes? With our yearly review process, we compare you to others in your industry and point out areas where your expenses are high."

Prospect: "Gosh, I don't know. I guess we could probably cut some expenses." **(FAT)**

You: "If you were to guess, how much fat do you suppose could be cut if you knew where you were high?"

Prospect: "Hard to tell." **(FAT. You need solid numbers!)**

You: "I'm sure it is indeed hard to tell. But a guess is okay. What do you think is possible?"

Prospect: "I'm sure we could be cutting about $100,000 in expenses each year."

Now, you test the prospect to find out if he's feeling enough economic pain at this point by saying something like, "That's not that much," or "How much would you have to save for it to make sense to solve the problem?"

> You: "So, what I'm hearing is that over the next few years, you're looking at a potential increase of sales of at least $250,000 just by better financing your yearly fluctuations and then another $100,000 each year in potential cost savings. That's about how much?"

> Prospect: "It's going to be more than $750,000."

> You (testing the water): "Now I don't want to assume that saving $750,000 is a big amount for a business of your size, but neither do I want to assume it's not. How do you feel about that?"

At this point, the prospect will go one of two ways:

- If he says, "Are you kidding me? Do you know what I could do with an extra $750,000!?" you know he has enough economic reason to choose you. You can move to the next stage.

- If he says, "Well, it's not that much," you know you need to delve more deeply, finding additional pain and adding the economics of that pain to your current figure.

If the prospect feels that $750,000 is substantial, you now know that the additional $10,000 in interest margin that you charge is small potatoes in comparison. This prospect has sold himself on the great savings that will occur by spending more with you!

Simply stated, your job is to help your prospects discover how much it costs them to **not** be your client and to find out if they have both the budget to fix the problem *and* the willingness to change. If you do your job well, you will shorten the buying cycle dramatically because your prospects see the cost of not being your customer.

The questions you use to build the economic case should begin with:

- "How much…?"
- "What percentage…?"
- "Have you ever…?"
- "Which is more important…?"

For example:

- "How much is it costing when that happens?"
- "What percentage of that are you comfortable spending to make sure it doesn't happen?"
- "Have you ever not taken the lowest price option?"
- "Which is more important, price or cost?"

If you are selling a 401(k) option, and your competitor doesn't visit your prospect annually for meetings with the employees to discuss options as a way of optimizing goodwill created by the availability of that benefit plan (this is one of your USPs), know that *there are real costs attached to the competitor's inaction*. Your job is to get the prospect to see those costs as well.

The costs could include:

- Employee turnover
- Employees making bad financial choices
- Lost opportunities for employee goodwill
- The cost of administration due to employees not understanding how the 401(k) plan works

A discussion about what the problem or pain is costing the prospect always precedes any discussion about a budget, the amount the prospect has *available* to spend, or about the price, the amount the prospect is *willing* to spend, to remove the pain. Prospects must first fully understand *what the problem or pain costs them*, so they have a frame of reference when the topic of the cost of fixing the problem is discussed later.

Example:

> In a recent conversation, a financial institution identified that not fixing its service and sales process was costing them *$4 million –$5 million* from their bottom line *each year* in missed opportunities. Also, with an aggressive competitor arriving in town, the institution estimated that if it did nothing to solve the problem, it would probably lose an additional *$3 million each year* from current profits. When looking at a *$7 million–$8 million* problem each year, it suddenly seemed foolish not to spend the money to solve the problem.

If you skip the stage that reveals the economics of the pain, rest assured that your prospect will have trouble with your pricing.

Now, in this stage of your sales call, after your prospects recognize how much their problem costs them, your goal is to guide them. Find and quantify the financial benefit of doing business with you. Find out how they will budget for your solution—the additional money they will be spending to ultimately *save them money*, and where they'll find that little extra amount that you'll charge. This step helps you determine if prospects are indeed in a situation to spend more to get your financial benefit. You need to know if they even have enough money, and if they do, are they are willing to spend it?

> Warning: **This is not a time to talk about what you charge.** What they can pay is *unrelated* to what you charge. Keep the focus on what their problems cost them, and then uncover what they're willing to pay. If you show your cards now, the game could be over.

Beware of prospects who love your solution but have absolutely no way to pay for it.

Example:

> A college kid, Joe, goes into the BMW dealership and starts talking to the salesperson, Sue. Sue is asking all the right questions about Joe's current "beater" car and is helping him uncover all his pain about not having the BMW. She goes into the BMW USPs, the superior performance, the excellent quality, the luxurious interior, the resale value, etc. Joe is sold on the car; he can justify the higher price, and has no problem paying more for getting more. So far, he has met all the qualifications, but before going to Sue's office to discuss the price, the different options, and to begin completing the paperwork, Sue asks some

questions about Joe's budget and where he will get the money for the car. She quickly finds out that Joe's pockets are not very deep—enough for a pizza and pop, maybe. She will not make a special "deal" or negotiate to lower the price because of Joe's current financial situation. Sue should not waste her time presenting to an unqualified prospect.

As you approach the budget part of the economics conversation, you can take a number of different avenues:

"In any area of your business, when you have had a problem that costs you $250,000, what have you been comfortable spending to fix it?"

Or:

"It has been our experience that some _____ solutions cost from $____ to $_____. Where in that spending range would you feel most comfortable investing to fix these issues?"

Or:

"Let me understand. You say this problem is costing you $10,000 per quarter. Are you committed to fixing it? If so, how much of that $10,000 are you willing to spend to see that bill disappear for good?"

Do not leave this step until you have an amount! If the prospect doesn't give you a number, your profit margins are going to take a beating.

If you ask, "How will you pay for the additional amount it costs to save you the $750,000?" and they say, "I don't know," that prospect has just given you a negative answer. You must meet them with a negative response, "Sounds like you don't have the means to fix the problem. What would you like me to do?" Get them to tell you why you should stay. If they can't, you should leave, saving yourself the wasted time and money. (This concept will be explained in greater detail in the section on the commitment stage.)

When you take your prospects through this sequence of economic questions, you gain awesome power. You've flipped them from being concerned about how much you charge to being focused on what it's costing them ***not*** to work with you.

STEP 4 OF PROFIT-RICH SALES:
EVALUATION & DECISION PROCESS

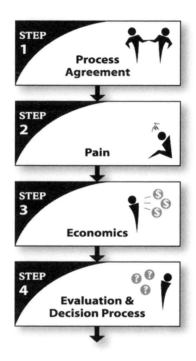

DECISION PROCESS GAME RULES:

PROTECTING YOURSELF FROM THOSE SHOCKING SURPRISES

L et's imagine that you're invited to play in a card game. You sit down with others at the table, the hands are dealt, and you are asked to throw your best card into the center. What do you do? How do you know what card to throw down? If you want any chance to do well, you will logically ask, "What game are we playing, and what are the rules?" And if you truly wanted a shot at victory, you'd probably follow with some questions to learn the objectives and the necessary strategy needed to win.

As a kid, you encountered this type of situation hundreds of times. When asked to play in a simple game, you handled it in much the same way every time. "What game are we playing, and what are the rules?" It was a no-brainer. You wanted to play, and the competitive drive in you wanted to win.

Yet, for some strange reason, when prospects ask salespeople to "play a game," salespeople eagerly begin playing without a complete understanding of the game and its rules. Remember, you learned as a kid that if you didn't know the game and understand the rules, you'd never win. This is no different in business.

You must get the prospect to share with you his or her process for evaluating an offer up front. If you miss this step in the process, all your hard work will be for nothing. *Don't let them tell you they don't have an evaluation process. They do!*

The only way you can find out the rules in any game is by asking. You must ask prospects to describe *in detail* their *process* for evaluating an offer; and have them tell you what determines whether they will accept an offer, and in what order all the necessary events will happen.

You can start by asking with something as straightforward as:

> "Please help me to understand the *evaluation and decision process* you or your company use to evaluate a proposal."

Make sure to use the word *process* in this initial request. While still important, you don't want to know *who* makes the decisions as much as you need to know *how* the decision is made. *Exactly what determines whether they will accept an offer* to do business with you?

The answer encompasses much more than just who makes the decision. Is Auntie Beth from Tulsa, who holds 51 percent of the company's stock, in on the deal? If so, she'll make her decisions on grounds that are different from those of the COO. You need to uncover *exactly* how the evaluation and decision process plays out. Remember, you can't win a game when you don't understand the rules.

You need to uncover the following elements of the process:

- Key players—*all* of them (any third parties, bosses, owners, advisors, committees, boards, etc.)

- Who don't you know yet who's in the picture?

- Who else is the prospect considering?

- What's the sequence of steps in the process?

- When will the necessary meetings take place?

- Who makes the final call?

- When will the decision be made?

Notice that finding out how the decision is made happens well *before* you put the actual offer on the table. You haven't shown any cards yet.

Begin by making your prospect understand that you are serious. If this conversation and relationship is going to go any further, the prospect also needs to be serious. You are setting the stage for your prospect's inevitable questions (including "Why can't I shop your proposal around?").

The most important things you need to understand about the evaluation and decision process are:

- Where in the process do you get points for your USP?

- When does the prospect want the pain to end?

- Who, of all the decision makers, is the tie breaker?

Unless you know the answers to these questions, you have no business quoting prices, presenting your proposal, or wasting time in any other way that puts you in a game you don't know how to win.

STEP 5 OF PROFIT-RICH SALES:
COMMITMENT

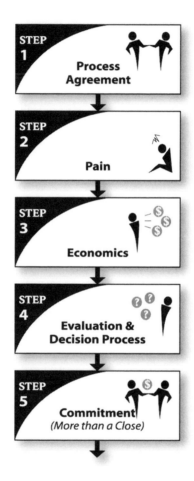

PILE OF MONEY MAGIC:
GET THE COMMITMENT BEFORE
YOU MAKE YOUR PROPOSAL

In order for the prospect to successfully complete your sales process, you *always* have to know what is going to happen next. At every cornerstone (the process agreement, the pain, the economics, the evaluation and decision process, and everything in between), your prospect *must commit to the next stage before moving forward*. Why continue blindly when the prospect may just be in it for the free information and free lunch? Your resources, time, knowledge, and experience are valuable! Prospects don't have a right to access any of this unless they tell you exactly what they are thinking at each stage of the process.

That said, below are three crucial commitments that will get you to the sale.

1. Agreement About Being Last to Present

You should not be surprised that your prospect is talking to several competitors. Research from a major multi-billion-dollar electronics manufacturer (with ten years of data and an 85 percent market share of their target area) found that in multi-vendor situations, *the salesperson who presents last is guaranteed the sale 94 percent of the time!* The mark of a good sales-person is not "wheeling and dealing," but rather mastering how to secure this profitable presentation position, especially when competing against an incumbent.

We often hear heartbreaking stories from people who took their best shot, had an agreement to do business, did all the paperwork, and put together the package, only to have the incumbent come back and revise their offer once they saw what the prospect was offered in the other proposals.

Does this sound familiar? Although you may have left the meeting on cloud nine because of how well it went, you must remember, yours was not the last presentation the evaluation committee heard. Who knows what your competitors had to offer—or what they said they could match?

While the prospective client may have loved your ideas and even commit-ted to your pricing, the person presenting after you stole the thunder—and with relative ease.

What went wrong? Simple: You were in no position to respond. By going last, your competitor was able to first, discuss *what you proposed*, and then, follow that up by *countering* that proposal.

In sales, you want your prospect to perceive you as the most unique competi-tor, the one providing the most value, and meeting more of their requirements than any other company. Tip the scales in your favor by putting yourself in this favorable position: present last.

- Share your appealing solution to ease their pain.
- Take ownership of the competitor's solution by adding your own twist.
- Remove the opportunity for a competitor to respond to your solution.

You have solved all their problems single-handedly. At this point, the competition can do nothing. And since you presented last, you've made the final positive impression on the prospect.

When do you secure this coveted position at the end of the line? Before you share your ideas.

> "Would there be any reason I couldn't be last?"
>
> "Would there be any reason I couldn't present after your current vendor?"

Be prepared to explain why you are making the request. Tell them you want to have a more level playing field after the incumbent takes their best shot. You know you have much more to offer them, and you want a chance to prove it.

Be forthright. You want to win their business, and the chance of winning that business increases if you present last. If they balk at that, find out why. If they tell you that their nephew, Eddie (who can't hold a job), gets to present last, what they're really saying is that you won't get this deal—no matter when you present. They're asking for unpaid consulting because Eddie could never figure out how to solve the company's problem on his own, but he can match a price.

If that's the case, save yourself the time and say, "Sounds like this deal is Eddie's." Then wait for their reaction. You will either get the deal in advance or you will save yourself the hassle of pretending that there still could be a deal.

Be assured that presenting last can raise your income while also reducing the number of hours you work. So if something changes and you have to give up your spot at the back of the line, don't present. This will save you time in the end.

Be prepared to work hard—very hard—in order to be last.

Testimony from Terry Slattery

I worked for a company when I was a young salesman that helped me to always be last. There used to be things called mainframe computers, and I sold them. They were very expensive transactions and my employer, the IBM Corporation, made it a *condition of employment* that you be last. You signed a contract to that effect the first business day of every New Year. In a multi-vendor competition that involved great expenditure of IBM's resources, *you had to be last* or you would be dismissed. So you can imagine how hard we fought for this critical position. It didn't take long for the competition to figure out that we had a strong motivation to be last, so they came up with their own tactics.

What I am referring to has become known as "The Dying Grandmother Move." So, we had to learn how to deal with the *competition's* grandmother dying the day before they were supposed to present, meaning, they would have to reschedule, which would put them last. For example, a competitor knew I was already promised the last spot, so he called in and said something about how one of the guys on the team had a grandmother who had taken seriously ill in Alaska, and this guy was the only one who could get into the cabin with the pack mules, and he had to leave last night. He was the one who knew everything about the presentation, so they were going to need to reschedule. This "Dying Grandmother Move" is very common in high-tech sales.

As part of us asking to be last, we also asked to be last no matter *whose* grandma went down. We actually developed a routine called "The Dying Grandmother Question Sequence" that we would take the prospect through, and we prayed that the competition would pull "The Dying Grandmother Move" because then they had no credibility.

The question sequence went as follows:

Me: "What is your process?"

Prospect: "We are going to bring in three finalists."

Me: "Assuming we make the finals, what has to happen for me to be last?"

Prospect: "Done. You'll be last; nobody else has asked."

Me: "Okay, can we agree to one other thing? When you assign the presentation sequence and I'm last, if somebody who's in front of me has a grandmother who dies, God forbid, but if she does go down, and they need to reschedule behind me, can we agree that I automatically move to last again, behind them?"

Then they would ask what I was talking about, and I would explain it to them. The prospect would ask me if they really do that, and then would say, "Well, if they do that, they are out."

Then all you have to do is pray that they call in with the grandma story.

So *you* need to be working just as hard to be last. After all, you rest the entire sale on this commitment.

2. Before You Present, Know What Happens After

You need your prospect to commit in advance, *before you propose,* as to what will happen *after* you have presented. This may cause you some discomfort, especially if you consider yourself a "people person," but it is extremely effective and important to the process. Proposals are expensive and inconvenient, so you must understand exactly what will happen after you have answered all of their questions. Introduce this subject to the prospect with something similar to the following statement:

> "Okay Mr. / Ms. Prospect, I want to make sure I understand exactly what's going to happen. If I present you a plan to take care of Pain 1 and Pain 2, and we also eliminate Pain 3 within the price range that you shared with me, and I've answered all your questions, what do you see yourself doing?"

By finding out what happens afterward, you have essentially closed the transaction. Your prospects must reveal how they will react to such an offer before you begin any efforts to put a deal together. You must get a clear, straight answer. Fat words are unacceptable!

"I'll take a hard look at it" doesn't count!

"We'll think it over" is not a commitment!

If you get any fat words, take the safest path: "I don't understand. Help me." You are missing something and have more work to do to get their commitment. If you have to go back to more pain questions or get a clearer understanding of their evaluation and decision process, do that now—*before* you present (at that point, it's too late).

To obtain the final commitment you must know:

- What happens after/if...?
- Would there be any reason the prospect couldn't ...?
- Can the prospect do what he says he will do?

3. Agree That It's Okay to Say "NO"

You need your prospects to commit to tell you "no" if they know at the end of your presentation that they do not intend to buy. This allows you to leave without false expectations that the opportunity is still alive.

You are looking for the prospect's "commitment." What does that mean? Commitment means they will take action and accept your offer to do business—or the discussion is done and you're not going to persist any further. You and the prospect have to be comfortable with either answer. By getting a commitment, you now have a clear resolution, and your business forecast begins to include some elements of reality. Beware of the "nice guy," the one who keeps you delusional about the idea of doing business but simply doesn't return your phone calls for weeks because he hasn't got the backbone to free you so you can move on. This is why you must make it known to your prospect that it is okay to say "no."

If you make sure each of these three commitments is agreed upon *before* presenting, the likelihood of walking away with an actual client rather than just a prospect is ten times greater.

GOLD MINE CALL PLANNING:
PREPARING FOR PREDICTABLE RESULTS

Too many salespeople make sales calls without giving a thought as to *why* they are going on the call, and what they hope to accomplish from it. It's amazing to hear the responses elicited from salespeople when asked *why* they're calling on the prospect. All the answers soon sound the same: "To see if they need me," or "To see if I can help them."

In reality, the purpose of the initial meeting with the prospect is to *qualify, qualify, and qualify.*

Unless you are in a one-call business, the initial conversation with a prospect should never include presenting offers. Never mention valuable information, such as rates and terms. Your purpose on the initial call is to begin the qualification or disqualification process—and that's it. This process includes several elements, some of which are:

- They tell you **they have reasons to change.**
- They tell you they are **comfortable spending more money** for your solution than what they are currently spending.

- **They have told you when** they would like to have their financial services relationship improved.

- **They have described their process for evaluating** a new financial services relationship.

- **They tell you** *exactly* **what happens** if you come back with an offer.

The call will most likely proceed along the following general lines:

1. You need to spend a couple of minutes building **rapport**. Then as soon as possible, you want to get the prospect to agree to your **communication process**. At this point, discuss the process agreement.

2. Then, move the prospect to **describing their reasons** for considering a new business relationship. Uncover their pain using the tools and questions described in previous chapters. This part of the conversation should consume approximately twenty to thirty minutes of the available time.

3. Methodically review the costs of the pain. Get the prospect to tell you the amount of money that's available and what they are willing to spend to get rid of the various pains.

4. Complete the qualification process by finding out the answers to the five points of qualification in the previous section. They **must meet all five points**, and if they can't or don't know the information, you need to know why—and then find out who *can* answer your questions.

When executed properly, you will have no time on an initial sales call for any extras, and certainly not any presentations. Before any meeting or phone call, think about how far into your process you expect to get, as well as the outcomes you are seeking. Practice with your co-workers first, following your notes until you get the hang of it. While on the call, you might feel the urge to skip over something because it might not seem important at the time. However, if you don't follow through on all the steps, the sale will never follow through, either. If you miss a step, it's okay to go back. (Late is better than never.)

STEP 6 OF
PROFIT-RICH SALES:
PRESENT

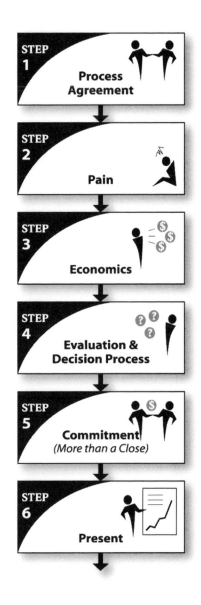

SHOWTIME:

UNBEATABLE PRESENTATIONS
TO CINCH THE DEAL

Okay, we've finally reached the point you've been itching to get to: the presentation. First, let's make sure you've got the details covered.

Pre-Presentation Checklist

Step 1: You identified the <u>Emotional Buyer</u>.

This is the person who is experiencing the most pain without your services and lies awake at night trying to figure out how to make the pain(s) go away.

Step 2: The Emotional Buyer has <u>told</u> you about the pains and consequences they have been experiencing without you.

The pains you uncovered were taken down to a minimum of three levels, to where the real truth was revealed.

You uncovered enough pain(s) for the prospect to be committed to change.

Step 3: You talked about the <u>economics of their pain</u>. The prospect has told you what the pains cost them and what they are willing to spend to fix the problems.

Step 4: You understand *exactly* how the <u>evaluation and decision process will occur.</u>

You know **all the key players.**

You know who breaks the ties.

You know all about the competition.

You know *exactly* when the decision will be made.

You understand where you get points for your USP.

Step 5: You've reviewed the <u>commitment</u> step.

You secured the last presentation slot—even if "Grandma goes down."

You have asked and you know what happens after you show them how you can fix the problem and present a solution with acceptable terms.

Congratulations! You've made it to the most anticipated point of every sale—**showtime!**

First, quickly review with your prospects the commitments the prospect made when scheduling the presentation.

You are presenting last. Remember, if "Grandma goes down," you have the right to reschedule. If you don't, the likelihood of your getting this deal will decrease dramatically.

All key players will attend the presentation.

Recap when they want the pain fixed and affirm that the date still stands.

Verify the time you've been given to present.

Your presentation will be brief and focused because you present only those products and services that are specific to the prospect's motives or pains. **Do not propose a solution for something the prospect has not indicated is a problem.** This only muddies the water. Keep it strictly to what they've asked for.

Plan on your presentation so that it takes only half the time allotted. This will leave time for you to deal with questions and any surprises.

When you start the presentation, begin with a review of the prospect's motives. Next, review the economic issues, the cost of the problem, and the terms the prospect's company is comfortable investing in the form of fees and pricing to fix it. Discuss all aspects of their process to evaluate and make a decision regarding your offer. Then, go over the commitment agreement you've made and review with them any adjustments to those agreements that need to be considered.

Before you propose your solutions, establish a "death to paradise" rating scale with your audience—0 to 10. Doing so will help you understand how close they are to saying "yes" to your solutions. The gauge works in the following manner:

Example:

> "I'd like to be able to know that I'm answering all of your questions throughout the presentation. I'll be asking you periodically how I'm doing on a scale of zero to ten, zero being "Nice try, but no cigar"—it's definitely not what you want—and ten being you envision the solution in place, saving you time and money."

Notice two things about this "death to paradise" scale. First, we used zero, not one, as your starting point. Zero allows your prospect the option to say "no." You are okay with the sale dying. This gives them an "out" and acknowledges that you're okay with a "no." Ten is more than just a "yes"; they can actually see your solutions in place and working for them—it's paradise.

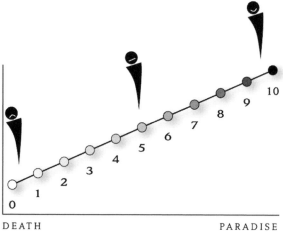

DEATH   PARADISE

When presenting your solutions, sequence it in the order most important to your prospect, according to what they've determined to be their most intense pain. Your presentation gets a warmer reception if it matches the prospect's priorities.

Here's an example:

> Assume you are fixing three problems for them: Problem 1, Problem 2, and Problem 3. Ask *them to pick* which of those three problems you address first. Then, present your solution to that problem. Test their reaction to this portion of your presentation with the 0-10 scale before you move on to the other two pains.

Go around the room and ask each person how that solution scored. You should hear nines and tens. If not, something wasn't clear. Go back and say, "Help me understand what would make it a ten?" With that information, you can clear up any misunderstandings or fuzziness. Don't move on to the next solution until you have a nine or ten from everyone. If you don't do it this way, you are setting yourself up for a "think-it-over" at the end. This is far and away the most successful format to use if you intend to walk out of the presentation with the business.

At the end of your presentation, when you've answered all their questions, ask:

"What do you want to happen next?"

At this point, you'll see that you've secured the business. They will most likely tell you that Nerdly (one of the support guys) is going to set up everything with you. Schedule the appointment then and there.

But wait, you're not quite finished. There is still one more crucial step remaining, and that's the after-sale confirmation. You want to make sure that your deal doesn't unravel when the announcement goes out to your competition that you were awarded the business. Seal it—for good!

Leave no stone unturned in the presentation. This is not a dog and pony show, nor is it a trial run. It is a time for prospects to commit to your solution unequivocally.

STEP 7 OF PROFIT-RICH SALES:
AFTER-SALE CONFIRMATION

16

Unshakable Commitment:

A Surprisingly Simple System to Ensure the Deal Won't Unravel

You handled the process well and have now been rewarded with the business. YIPPEE! You want to ring the bell and celebrate your success, but wait. You still have one last critical step to cinch this deal. You have to confirm the sale. You need confirmation from your prospects that they will follow through on their commitment before you can confidently refer to them as your client.

The prospect will always call the winner first—that's simply human nature. They want to delay making uncomfortable calls for as long as possible; no one likes to deliver bad news. Inevitably, though, they will have to call the losers of this beauty pageant. How do you think your competitors will react?

Your prospect may or may not be aware that the competitor will offer a last-minute proposal to save themselves. The gloves will come off, and the final swings to save this deal will begin. It's a mad race to match, undercut, and give away the farm, so you must make sure your prospect doesn't take the bait. You must rehearse the whole scenario with your prospects so they are not surprised and unprepared, but instead are *fully aware* of what is taking place. They should be able to actually *anticipate* the competitor's last-ditch effort, and be *ready* with a strong response to lay the competitor to rest for good!

What are the steps to the confirmation?

- **Prepare** your prospect to react to a last-minute pitch from the competition without wimping out. Everyone knows that the incumbent will not just step aside without a fight, and you have to be prepared for that. Be sensitive to the cues that reveal how the prospect feels about the competitor. This information will help you guide the prospect through the process of telling the competitor they're through.

- **Re-establish the prospect's commitment** to you. Remind them why they are choosing you. Discuss again the reasons and the pains they are experiencing and how you will fix them. Review the reasons why a last-minute price lowering from a competitor does not solve the problems they are having, it just covers them up.

Solidify the prospect's commitment by asking:

"You don't see the competitor's last swing working, right?"

"You don't see yourself getting turned around, do you?"

"You know that the other guys are going to try to drop their price, but do you remember what we talked about: *value* versus price?"

"How to do you see yourself reacting to their move?"

When your prospect tells you what they are going to do, they hear themselves saying it out loud, which programs them to give that response. By setting this up ahead of time, there are no questions about how your prospect will react when the competitor executes a last-minute play to save the deal.

- **Rehearse** your prospect to properly handle the desperate pitch from the other guys. Make them aware of how the competitors will react when they get the news and give them tools to deliver their response. Prepare your prospects for the counterattack and help them practice what they will do and say when it happens.

Ask the prospect the following:

"What do you think the reaction of the competitor will be when they find out? What are you going to do?"

Give them tools—the following phrases— with which to respond:

"We're not considering any other offers."

"Sorry it didn't turn out for you."

"We've made our decision, and it is final."

"It's too late."

"We're not looking at any more proposals."

These tools help your prospect *automatically* reply to the competitor. By putting the prospect on autopilot, they have no time to look at and think about the last-minute deal your competitor brings to the table. They are programmed to respond so that your competitor doesn't even have a chance to present a counteroffer.

You must go through this final after-sale confirmation step to ensure that all your hard work is not lost. If you allow the prospect to give way to this desperate effort by another competitor, your advantage as the final presenter will be taken away, and the possibility of this deal unraveling will increase—greatly. Think of how hard you've worked to keep your clients from going to a competitor. Realize also what you and your prospect are up against. If you both are prepared, and you have your prospect's commitment, only one team will score—yours!

WHEN IT DIDN'T WORK:
CONDUCTING THE AUTOPSY

Your prospects have been taken from A to Z in the sales process, nodding their head in agreement the whole way. Things looked good, but you still didn't get the sale. Not all is lost—here is still a way for you to win.

The sales dance between you and your prospects is nerve-racking. They are just as apprehensive about saying "no" as you are about hearing it. The rejection might sting for a minute (it always does), but remember, you said it was okay for them to say "no." Consider the position the two of you are in now. The pressure is gone. The decision has been made. You must have missed something that prevented you from uncovering the truth; now you can find out what that was.

What better time to uncover the real reasons your prospect was holding back than after the sale has been lost? They are no longer anxious, thinking about how they are going to let you down easily.

Get feedback on your sales performance—directly from the person who made the decision not to do business with you. Find out why your USP was not perceived as valuable. Conduct a follow-up call to find out what went wrong.

First, address the reason for the call and then move forward. Let them know from the start that you simply want to find out what you can learn from your past relationship—assure them that you aren't still trying to sell to them. Be professional, curious, and responsive.

Example:

> "Hi, this is Bill from _____. My role here is _____.
>
> The purpose of my call is to get some feedback on how we performed in addressing your recent _____. We don't seem to learn much from the ones we win, so I like to explore the ones where we got the bronze medal to find out what we need to work on. [Try to position this at the personal level so that it is harder for the former prospect to say "no" to the next question]. I realize that you're busy, but I have just a couple brief questions, if you have time to talk."

Next, ask the questions that get to the heart of the matter: where you went wrong:

1. This is a quality-audit type question: "Overall, how did our team perform?" You could give them cues as to what exactly you want to know, or let them answer spontaneously, without any further guidance or direction from you.

2. "What did we overlook in addressing your requirements?"

3. "What could we have done more effectively to help your team reach a decision?"

Emphasize how much you appreciate their input.

> "Thanks very much for your time, and please feel free to contact me anytime. If I could get your e-mail address, I'll send my thank you. I'll include my contact information again, so you'll have it should you need it in the future."

By the end of your call, you have created a higher-level relationship with the prospect than just being the salesperson who lost. You can use this to your advantage in the future. Whether it is the information you were able to get and use, *or* the relationship itself, you have created something that most haven't. All is **not** lost when losing the sale.

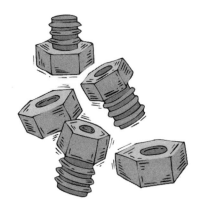

THE NUTS AND BOLTS OF PROFIT-RICH SALES

BIG MONEY MESSAGES:
VOICE MAIL STRATEGIES THAT GET BUSINESS

You know how a call with a prospect should go: how to start, what to ask, etc. But *how do you get to that first conversation?* After consulting with three different companies over a three-year period and monitoring over 600,000 calls, we found that about 92 percent of all business calls go to voice mail. Obviously, you need a strategy to cover this area.

The following are tips for effective voice mail messages:

- Limit yourself to a twenty-second maximum.
- Don't rush your phone number—say it slowly.
- Don't give them your live phone number; send them to your special voice mail (see below).
- Practice the message into your own voice mail box, timing it.
- Wait three to four business days between messages.

- Friday afternoon is the best time to call; this is when executives and owners are most likely in the office finishing up any loose ends.

Our studies have shown that *the phone number you give them to call you back should automatically go to voice mail.* But *not* to your normal voice mail, which says, "Hi, this is so and so at whatever company and I'm un-available at the moment, but if you leave a message, I will call you back as soon as possible." No, you need to have a separate voice mail just for your prospects that simply states:

> "Hi, this is Pat Jones. Please leave your name, company, and phone number—along with two times you can be reached. Thank you."

If you give them your live phone number, inevitably they'll call at the worst possible time. By sending the call to your "special" prospect voice mail, you gain control of when that call takes place so you can be prepared for the conversation.

Notice that on the outgoing message of the special voice mail, you don't leave your company name. This prevents your prospect from looking you up and potentially not returning future messages. It also keeps them curious as to who you are and what you can offer.

The voice mail messages should include several key points.

Message 1:

- *"Hi, Tom, this is Pat Jones."*

  "hello" and your name; don't reveal the name of your company

- *"I'm not sure if we ever need to talk in person."*

  negative opener

- *"I deal with executives who are concerned about the high risks of a mismanaged employee benefits program."*

  introduce pain #1

- *"I can be reached at ###-###-####."*

  leave your contact info., repeat your number twice, speaking slowly and clearly

- *"If you get my voice mail, please leave two different times when I can reach you, and I'll call you at one of them."*

  tell them what you want them to do if they call you back and get your voice mail

Message 2: (after three or four business days)

- *"Hi, Tom, it's Pat Jones."*

  "hello" and name; still no company

- *"I'm not sure if my call is even appropriate."*

  different negative opener

- *"You may not remember my previous call when I mentioned that the companies I talk to are commonly experiencing a strong concern about the high risks of a mismanaged employee bemefits program..."*

  review pain #1

- *"which means you may be more concerned about reducing the excessive employer costs in managing an employee benefits program."*

  introduce pain #2

- *"If you're interested, please call me at..."*

  leave contact info and instructions for voice mail

Message 3: (after three or four business days)

- *"Hi, Tom, it's Pat."*

  "hello" and name

- *"I'm really not sure if I can help you, and you may not remember my previous call when I mentioned..."*

  different negative opener

- *"reducing excessive employer costs in managing an employee benefits program."*

  review pain #2

- *"You may not be experiencing high costs, which means you are probably more concerned about the inflexibility of your employee benefit offerings."*

  introduce pain #3

- *"If you are interested in that, please call me at ..."*

  contact info and instructions

"Magic" Message #4:
(Again after three to four business days)

This is the last one and the one that gets the most returns.

- *"Hi, Tom, it's Pat."*
  "hello" and name

- *"I know you're busy and get a lot of calls, so you probably don't remember my last call about..."*

  negative opener

  "the inflexibility of your employee benefit offerings..."
  review pain #3

- *"which usually means you're not interested and I should close your file."*
  tell them you are going away, dropping their name, and closing out their file

- *"If that's <u>not</u> what you want, please call me by Friday at..."*
  leave contact info and give instructions

There is something magical about letting people know you're going away that seems to make them think that since you value your time, they should, too.

Finally, remember to speak slowly and clearly, and commit to following through with all four messages. Remember, it's the last call that gets the most returns!

2+2=4:
FOLLOWING THE FORMULA TO GUARANTEED RESULTS

Too many salespeople fail because they don't understand the recipe for success. Consider a salesperson who wants to close one piece of business for $25,000. If her closing percentage is only 50 percent (which means she's not very good), she would have to offer two proposals in order to close on one piece of business. In order to shake down her prospect list and disqualify those who don't make the cut, she might have to approach forty different prospects to get twelve initial discussion appointments. We call this "the sales funnel." Think of cooking and how you sift through the flour to get rid of all the bad bits and pieces that don't belong—until you are left with only the finest grain: the buying prospects! If you know what it takes to get one sale, you can figure what your workweek is going to look like for the whole year.

Calculate your average recipe for one sale. This recipe will be different for each person, depending on the quality of the leads they pursue and how good they are at closing.

For example:

Formula For One Sale (not fixed)

Now multiply the numbers in the formula by the number of sales you seek. If you need to close sixty sales in the year, you can multiply all the numbers by sixty. Next, break down the numbers by the month, the week, and the day. This way you will always have a good idea of where you are (remember the importance of situational awareness?). With your year's goals broken down in a recipe, you can easily calculate the number of approaches you need to make each day. For example, in the above figure, if the salesperson needed to close sixty sales per year, his cookbook would look like this:

Yearly	Monthly	Weekly	Daily
2400 New approaches	200 New approaches	50 New approaches	7.14 New approaches
720 Initial discussions	**60 Initial discussions**	**15 Initial discussions**	**2.14 Initial discussions**
300 Qualified prospects	25 Qualified prospects	6.25 Qualified prospects	.89 Qualified prospects
120 Offers	10 Offers	2.5 Offers	.36 Offers
60 Sales	5 Sales	1.25 Sales	.18 Sales

Keep in mind that everyone's cookbook will be different. Those who are better at closing will craft a different personal cookbook. If you follow the process for Profit-Rich Sales, you should expect a personal closing ratio of 90 percent. If you are a manager, you should hold your people accountable to a closing ratio of 90 percent. Anything less than 90 percent means too much time and effort is going into unqualified prospects.

As you become more comfortable with the Profit-Rich Sales System, you will discover that you're spending more time on the *right* prospects and you're closing more deals with higher profit margins. When you narrow your funnel by improving your closing ratio, you don't have to put in as many approaches to get the same number of sales!

Profit-Rich Prospecting

Nothing, absolutely nothing, is worse than cold calling on strangers who see you as a peddler. In fact, it's the worst use of your business development time, and it will eat up your profits if you get *any* business at all.

Smart people use their time wisely. If you call on prospects who have a high chance of loving what you do *and* have the ability to add profit margin to your business, you're on the path to using the only resource that is the great leveler—time.

Think of it this way: Some prospects and customers are "your people," and some clearly are "not your people." If you offer high-end solutions, the people willing to pay for your type of services are "your people." People who are simply looking for the best deal are "not your people." Not only do you waste time calling on people in the latter category, but time spent calling on them will surely demoralize you. If you're not very vigilant, your self-esteem will take a blow as you begin to realize that you treat your dog better than those prospects treat you. Additionally, if prospects are "not your people," and you do end up with a deal, they won't enable you to have any profit.

So first look at your current client base to see exactly how many of them qualify as "your people." We'll bet it's about 20 percent, and here's how we know.

In 1906, an Italian economist named Vilfredo Pareto observed that 20 percent of Italy's adult population owned 80 percent of the country's wealth. That was a startling find! Apparently, input is NOT equal to output.

Many years later in the United States, quality control guru Dr. Joseph M. Juran observed that quality defects were unequal in their frequency. This same phenomenon, which Juran called "The Vital Few and Trivial Many," also existed with respect to most every component of business. Additionally, it's a concept that all successful people understand how to use. Today we call it the "80/20 Rule," or the "Pareto Principle." This principle states:

Twenty percent of our clients give us 80 percent of our profits.

- *Twenty percent of our projects will give us 80 percent of our results.*
- *Eighty percent of a problem can be solved by identifying the correct 20 percent of the issues.*

To clear up a common misperception, Pareto, didn't create this principle, Juran did. Juran just chose to name it after Pareto.

So, to have a healthy sales funnel, you must have a healthy marketing funnel that attracts the desired prospects—those who resemble the 20 percent of your client base considered "your people." As a dear friend of Roxanne's who was a marketing expert in healthcare said after her divorce, "I plan to remarry, and I see this as an easy task. Looking for a husband is just like marketing. You have to find lots of prospects and then quickly disqualify them."

Although this strange relationship approach didn't resemble a traditional approach, Roxanne's friend was right in her observation. Most people don't remarry because they spend too much time trying to make a relationship work with someone who was never suitable as a marriage partner in the first place, instead of moving on and finding someone who is. Many spend years with someone they know they could never marry. Sound familiar? Like when you spend countless hours of your professional life presenting to unqualified prospects?

Remember the sales funnel described in the previous chapter and think of a similar marketing funnel filled with all your potential prospects. Thousands and thousands of people who could become your clients wait at the top of the funnel. Obviously, you don't have enough time or resources to contact all of them, and many of them wouldn't be a source of lucrative business anyway.

You must narrow this group to more focused prospects.

ABC CLIENTS

To start this funneling process, you first need a system to handle your current clients. Assign a code to every current client: "A," "B," or "C."

A is for all the clients who fall within the top *20 percent of profitability*. (And, no, you can't have 40 percent of your clients in your 20 percent category.)

C is for the *bottom 20 percent*—all the clients who take the profits right out of your bottom line and have little to no hope of ever becoming "A" clients.

All those remaining are coded **B.** But, leaving a client in the "B" category is not an option.

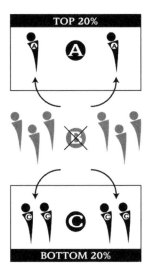

Each salesperson should review and contact all their assigned "B" accounts within six to twelve months to develop action plans to turn these accounts into either "A" or "C" accounts. By assigning the "ABC" codes, you narrow your focus to quality clients ONLY. Now that you have identified your quality clients, find a list of prospects just like them.

Minnesota's most sought-after fish is the walleye. The walleye is never seen swimming with a school of trout. Walleye naturally unite because they eat the same things, live in the same places, and make the same friends and enemies. Is there a metaphor here?

Think of your hot prospects as the esteemed walleye. Your prospects may not all eat at the same restaurants, but they can be found congregating together at the same places. "A" clients sing your praises to "A" prospects and suddenly, instead of cold-calling "C" clients, you're handling the referrals from "A" clients. Since "A" clients tend to spend time with "A" prospects, you're now leveraging your time by working with prospects who have high profit potential.

To arrive at a list of these hot prospects, look at your current list of profitable clients and find prospects who have commonalities.

Analyze your top 20 percent of clients ("your people") to find out what they have in common. As a result of this review, you discover that 50 percent belong to Swing and Miss Golf Club, 40 percent live in the Cherry Hill estates area, and 75 percent own manufacturing firms with annual revenue of $4 million to $20 million. At this point, you have a start to your mailing list. All you need to do is buy the golf club list, go to a mail house company to buy the list of homeowners in Cherry Hills, and obtain a list of local manufacturers with the level of revenue you are looking for. Easily done.

Probably fewer than 1,000 people actually belong on your list of prospects to contact on a regular basis. With this group, give, give, and give some more—both information and help. They will be so taken aback by the fact that you're not selling them or sending them sales brochures (leave those low-achieving tactics to the competition) that when they get the chance to do business with you, they'll jump at the opportunity to find out what makes this "giver" tick.

To become the "giver," you need to mail and mail and mail. Focus on value for the prospect—not on promoting your "stuff." (i.e., your agenda). But make it obvious the mailing *came* from you. They'll be so thrilled to receive your mailings that they will come to count on the valuable information you provide.

The best way to start the relationship with potential prospects is to have a mail piece that requires their attention—and action.

For example:

> "Please return this postcard if you are interested in having your staff attend a seminar on saving hours of needless accounting by integrating Bill Pay with your current accounting software."

If they send back a card with the "interested" box checked, you have a warm lead looking forward to becoming a hot lead.

Other mailings could include:

- Ten tips for organizing your next tax year
- Seven habits of people who accumulate wealth
- New tax law changes that could impact your retirement
- Why your manufacturing firm may be better off as a Sub S
- Invitations to VIP events
- Invitations to seminars

When you continually send prospects helpful information, you create new friends who are receptive to your ideas, making it easy for the potential prospects to become hot leads.

From your mailing list of 1,000, target about 100—these will be the prospects who responded to your mailings. Move them through the sales funnel with the objective of either having them become a client or taking them off your dance card. The idea is to have 100 percent of these top 100 prospects resemble the top 20 percent of your clients so that you are always dealing with "your people."

You can call on these people, send them more detailed information, and give them additional attention.

This list, you will notice, is extremely qualified; the people on it resemble your most profitable clients—and the clients who already love what you do. Calls to this group feel comfortable; they are "your people." Marketing to "achievers" means they will be thrilled to do business with a financial services provider who deals with *other* achievers.

The remaining 900 prospects on your mailing list continue to hear from you until they demonstrate signs of interest and you move them into the sales funnel, or until it is clear that they are not interested. Remove those not interested from your list. It is important to continually assess the changing characteristics of "your people" so that you can constantly update your mailing list and gain access to more and more potential prospects.

By keeping your marketing funnel full, you will have far better qualified sales leads. The more prospects you have, the easier you'll find it to stand firm on your pricing, because you know that if you lose one, another will follow right behind.

TEN TIMES MULTIPLIER:
THE ENLIGHTENED PATH TO WEALTH

What's the biggest mistake low-performing salespeople make?

They don't understand "use value," a term coined by Wallace Wattles in his book *The Science of Getting Rich*. Knowing what use value is and how to use it is the most important part of the foundation for successful sales.

Use value means that people feel that by simply associating with you, they will gain value for themselves beyond their cost. And people will always migrate to where they feel they receive increased value.

"Always seek to give ten times the use value compared to the cash value you receive."

Now, before you start thinking this means you give away the farm, stop. Exactly the opposite is true. You should, in fact, *get* the whole farm, because you are giving your client what *feels* like the whole state. No one has ever built a successful business by trying to do an even swap.

Go **way** beyond the commodity you are selling to offer such extraordinary value that it doesn't make sense for the prospect to go anywhere else for the service.

Consider the following examples:

If a prospect wants a CD, a low performer will quote the rates and only get the business if they have the best rate. Alternatively, giving ten times use value looks like this:

> "I would love to share our rates with you. Before I do, I want to make sure we're giving you the best advice so we're not hurting you by investing your funds in the wrong instrument. Let me ask some questions to find out what you're trying to accomplish and how you're currently trying to get there."

Then request a list of all their CDs, including the maturities, institutions where they're held, and all the corresponding rates. Discuss laddering the CDs so the person can get the best returns while maintaining the ability to access the money if there is an unexpected need.

Find out what they're saving for, and if appropriate, encourage them to invest in CDs they can add to, CDs that change rates, or whatever the appropriate recommendation is, based on what they tell you they need. When you're finished asking questions, tell the client that rates shouldn't be a concern—because yours *are* competitive. This allows them to understand that you aren't skirting the issue of pricing (but you're minimizing its importance).

Remind them that, to keep things simple, they need to have a program and system to effectively manage their monies under one roof. Make sure they receive the best value for the long run.

At this point, tell them you want to help them even more. Show them a form they can sign to transfer each CD, and explain that you'll send the signed form to the financial institution that currently holds the CD. Describe for the client how the money in the CD will be automatically sent to you, their advisor, at the maturity date. Tell the client you'll call them on each of those dates to provide laddering suggestions that will fit their financial plan.

Now, *that's* **use value.**

If someone is looking for a mortgage, and you just quote the rate, you've delivered no use value. Most people approach mortgages incorrectly, only shopping for rates and getting the wrong program—paying too much in fees and interest. Instead, tell them about the hundreds of options available for current configurations and approaches to mortgages. Let them know you will ask them several questions and guide them to the mortgage best suited for them. **That's use value!**

By giving more in value than what you receive in cash, you will gain a strong reputation for excellence with your current clients—and the word will also spread to potential clients.

CONQUERING YOURSELF:
GOING TO WAR WITH YOUR MENTAL ROADBLOCKS

According to T. Harv Eker in *Secrets of the Millionaire Mind: Mastering the Inner Game of Wealth,* 80 percent of people who win the lottery file for bankruptcy within five years. Five years! How could that be? Buckets of extra cash all gone with nothing to show for it? It's because the winners don't have the necessary money consciousness to handle great wealth before they win the money, as evidenced by their level of income prior to winning the lottery. And since it is our consciousness that gives us our results—no exceptions—the winners are not able to hang on to their new-found riches.

If you get more money than you think you deserve, you *will* sabotage your results. Have you ever noticed how often salespeople start having an outrageously good year, only to end it with some debacle that sabotages the entire year's result? Their consciousness did not keep pace with their results. Simply stated, results must always align with consciousness.

You've learned the tools and processes necessary to create outstanding sales results, but now you must be willing to change the way you think and act in order for those results to really stick. Don't let yourself, your current behaviors, feelings—or your beliefs or way of thinking—get in the way of your enjoyment of your "lottery winnings."

Results come from feelings, which come from our behaviors. Behaviors come from programming, or what we think of as our beliefs. If you want to change your results, you *must* alter the programming in your mind.

In fact, most of our beliefs are not really *our* beliefs at all. We inherit beliefs very early in life from those who influence us. That's why Catholics raise little Catholics. Methodists raise little Methodists. Republicans raise little Republicans. You get the point.

In order to function fully as a highly successful human, you have to look at all your beliefs and find out if you really do believe them. Analyze which of your current beliefs serve you, and which ones harm you.

Salespeople have all kinds of beliefs. Some serve them well; others don't. We've all experienced "cold call anxiety," "title fear," and "the need for approval." Ernie Larsen, an internationally recognized author and teacher on building self-confidence, developing healthy relationships, and overcoming various compulsive behaviors, has developed numerous ideas about overcoming these limitations. The diagram below illustrates the link between our beliefs, our behaviors, our feelings, our results, and ourselves.

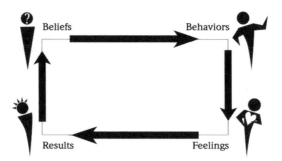

Salespeople come to a position with a set of beliefs about themselves. Those beliefs might not be truthful, but they are unquestioned. For example, a salesperson might believe, "I don't like to prospect," or "Don't talk to strangers," or "Don't ask questions," or "Don't talk about money." The beliefs you harbor set boundaries for the behaviors you choose in your work. So, if your belief system says, "I don't like to prospect," you will have a very small set of behavioral options available to use when it is time to prospect—and you won't even use those much.

Behaviors are always based on beliefs. Say you attend a certain training program or read a self-improvement book. As a result, you attempt to modify your behavior in an effort to achieve only one thing: increase your performance. Hence, you doom yourself to short-term improvement followed by regression. Doing what feels comfortable and fits with your beliefs is a natural tendency. Why? Because if you have not changed your beliefs, feelings of discomfort will always accompany the behaviors that occur outside of your beliefs. And although the behaviors within your belief system may not deliver anything close to the results you seek, desire, and deserve, you will continue to do them because they are "comfortable."

Obviously, behavior and the subsequent results are joined at the hip. If your behaviors prove not to create the results you seek, then your results will disappoint you. This will then subconsciously reinforce the belief system that's holding you back in the first place. This scenario plays out again and again and again.

However, once you understand the principles involved, you can change your beliefs, and you will see results quickly. If you want to change your current results, recognize when you are too deep in your comfort zone—and then figure out what you must do to change that.

If you think your beliefs might be holding you back, start by looking at the results in some area of your sales that you would like to change. Find the behavior and the belief responsible. For example, if you are not opening enough new accounts (the result), and you hate talking on the phone (the feeling), you may not be talking to enough people in a day (the behavior) because you believe cold calling stinks (the belief). You may believe, "I don't like to prospect." How do you think that that belief and subsequent behavior will show up in your work? Chances are you will have a negative feeling and will do little prospecting—or *barely enough* to survive. You certainly won't thrive.

Remember that your results are based on your feelings, your feelings are based on your behaviors, and your behaviors are based on your beliefs. **Not** doing something is as much a form of behavior as actually **doing** something, and both produce results—positive and negative. Therefore, you must identify the behaviors you do and don't do that create the results you experience.

Short-Term Reprogramming with Long-Term Results

You picked up almost all of your beliefs system by the time you were in first grade. At that point, you took ownership of your beliefs and didn't even question whether they were truthful or good for you. You learned to believe things like "Don't talk to strangers" and "Don't brag about yourself." These beliefs worked well then. Unfortunately, when you got older, you didn't erase them.

Now you are in sales and reluctant to pick up the phone and make a perfectly legitimate business approach to a valid prospect—all because of what you learned to believe at age five. You *can change* any of the non-supportive beliefs you have and thereby sell more consistently to get the results you want.

Many times people will try to change these beliefs with a "crash and burn" prospecting mode for a day, and expect to change the results without changing their beliefs. This never works, and eventually the person becomes worn out and gives up all together.

If you want to change your results, you must first be aware of your feelings and establish ownership of the behavior. Once you do that, ask yourself, "What do I believe about myself or this process of ____ (prospecting, cold calling, meeting people, etc.) that causes me to act this way?" Pick up the phone or go into a cold call and listen to all the internal self-talk you hear as you approach doing the actual behavior you don't like to do. That internal self-talk comes to you from your emotional thermostat.

You will quickly notice that your emotional thermostat sends out all kinds of disquieting signals and stressful feelings. It senses when you cross one of the protected behavioral boundaries and launch into something it knows you don't like to do. The thermostat tries to protect you, but in this case, it impedes the process—and progress. Recognize the behaviors and then dig underneath them to figure out what belief system you are acting on that causes you to under-perform.

The key to changing a salesperson's performance in any area begins with changing the belief system, and then adopting a new behavioral model leading to a positive change in their feelings. Understand that it will take *several weeks of discipline and effort* before the new beliefs take effect and a new level of more productive behavior emerges.

So how do you get there? You need to think about the results you want and the behaviors to accomplish them. Make a list of both, and then look at the behaviors. Which ones on the list do you wish would be minimized or disappear altogether? Which ones make you sick to your stomach? What is it that you believe that makes these behaviors so distasteful and causes your knees to buckle? The belief that just popped into your head—that's it. That nasty little culprit prevents you from achieving the results you want and deserve. Let's get rid of it.

First, take a look at how to install a new belief system. Write out a new version of the belief system you would like to have about yourself. It must be short, personal, and in the present tense. An affirmation like this can do a lot to reprogram your brain if it has a strong emotional component.

Here's an example:

> Instead of, "I need the prospect to like me," you might
> say, "I am joyfully conducting myself professionally, and
> I provide all the approval I'll ever need."

Notice that it's short and positive. It is in the present tense and it does not say anything about what you're trying to remove from your emotional thermostat. Write this down on a note card, say it out loud to yourself several times a day, and post it in your office so you see it frequently. After approximately *100 imprints* of this message, your emotional thermostat will begin to reset. As you affirm the new belief, you must also begin to do the corresponding behaviors **even though they are extremely uncomfortable!** After enough repetitions, your behavior will change permanently and higher production will follow. However, if you only affirm the new beliefs, but never actually *change to new behaviors*, you will never get the results you seek.

The discomfort will be temporary—typically three to four weeks. Your emotional thermostat will do everything it can to protect the old belief: "I need my customers to like me," because it has not yet taken ownership of the new belief: "I provide my own approval."

But most people quit just before the new imprinting takes root and delivers the desired result, because at this point the emotional thermostat delivers the greatest amount of discomfort. Instead of thinking, "This is never going to work," know that your brain is about ready to let it go—once and for all. Your belief system makes a last stand before surrendering. Stick it out, and the next thing you know your emotional thermostat will reset and the new beliefs will be as protected as the old ones were. Your beliefs will now be able to drive the right balance of sales behaviors. This process has worked well for thousands of people, and it will also work for you!

Review:

1. List the new results you want to achieve.

2. Identify the results you don't like.

3. Be brutally honest with yourself about the behaviors you do and don't do that create the results you don't like.

4. Figure out the underlying beliefs about yourself that you act out with inappropriate or non-productive behaviors. If you have trouble figuring it out, attempt the behavior. Take note of the message you receive from your emotional thermostat in the form of your internal self-talk.

5. Write out the belief system you would like to have governing your performance.

6. Read it out loud several times a day. At the same time, see yourself doing it successfully and enjoying it. The combination of saying it out loud, seeing it in your

mind, and feeling victory combine to create powerful, effective change.

7. At the same time you are reprogramming your mind, you must be doing the new behaviors. After all, it's the behaviors that physically produce the desired results.

For additional information on this topic, consult any of these books and resources, among others:

- *The Power of Your Subconscious Mind* by Joseph Murphy
- *Success Principles* by Jack Canfield
- *Learned Optimism* by Martin Seligmann
- If you're interested in resetting your thermostat, visit our website at www.EmmerichFinancial.com and review the information on the **PERMISSION TO BE EXTRAORDINARY** seminar.

THE WHOLE SHEBANG:
THE TEN NO-FAIL RULES
FOR PROFIT-RICH SALES

A t this point you should be really inspired to play the game of sales! And now you have an advantage because it's no longer a game where you don't know the rules. You have the rules clearly spelled out for you, and you know how to win the deal with premium pricing.

Understanding the process your prospects use to make decisions and where in that process you get points for *being better, rather than just being cheaper* helps you win the game.

Just as a football player running the wrong way has little likelihood of winning the game, so too are your chances if you're unprepared. You need to know the direction of the goal, and you need to have the right equipment.

We have shown you a step-by-step process to help you maneuver the field and get you to the goal line. Follow this process and these Ten Rules of Profit-Rich Sales, and you will win the game over and over again.

No-Fail Rule # I:
There are no free moves (This is the most important rule).

This basic principle from Economics 101 essentially says that all decisions have consequences, and every consequence comes with a cost. The costs can range from minute to very large. At any point, whatever decision you make will either cause something to occur, with the cost being the what you gain, or prevent something from occurring, with the cost being what you will lose from that "something" not occurring. A decision not to do business with you must have a *significant consequence*, or not doing business with you is the right move for the prospect. Get comfortable with the idea that every move you and your prospect make has a consequence and a cost. This principle operates in all areas of business and life:

- A computer chip that runs fast won't last very long because of the higher temperature created at the higher speeds.
- If you eat fast food every night, you will not lose weight.
- If you lift weights consistently, you will gain muscle tissue.

Likewise, if one of your prospects finds a lower rate for their mortgage from a large online institution, they may or may not be aware of the consequences of that choice. Do they know about the twenty-minute hold times they could face when trying to talk to someone about their account? Are they comfortable with different reps handling their account or having to reeducate the new rep of their situation each time they call? You must make these consequences perfectly clear to the prospect with questions—not declarative sentences.

No-Fail Rule # 2:
When the prospect goes negative—so do you.

When prospects are negative about the likelihood of doing business with you, you must be equally negative about the likelihood of doing business with them. By "going negative," you are actually removing confrontation. The door is now open for prospects to get on your side and help you find a way to continue talking.

You are never negative about the prospect or his or her process, only about the possibility of your being successful doing business with them. Nothing puts you in a worse position than appearing to be more committed to the sale than the prospect.

No-Fail Rule # 3:
Every time a prospect asks you to do anything that involves work or expenditure of you and your company's resources, know EXACTLY what will happen next before you do anything.

You must have an agreement before doing work requested by the prospect. (e.g., research, providing solutions, sending information, or giving a quote or proposal).

Before you do anything, make sure you know EXACTLY what happens after you do it. That word "exactly" means no guessing, no conditionals, no possibly's, no maybe's, no if's, no taking a look at, and no consideration. No more unpaid consulting! You don't want to show your prospects how you are going to fix the problem until they have told you what they are going to do if you show them.

No-Fail Rule # 4:
Drive the result of every sales call into one of the following three categories:

1. Mutual "no"

You both decide it doesn't make sense to continue. If you're not going to do business, find out early in the process so you can move on to productive calls.

2. Mutual "yes"

You both decide to continue pursuing the relationship by moving to the next step in your process.

3. Time Trap

You both know and agree that you are waiting for some event before the next steps are possible; this temporary situation is acceptable to both of you.

If you don't get one of the first three, you usually get the fourth option:

4. Continued Professional Education (CPE)—You get an education.

If you didn't achieve one of the first three outcomes you have no understanding of the relationship's potential, which puts you in a weak position.

The fact that you're getting an education instead of a deal clearly indicates that you skipped one of the sales steps. As a result, you end up in a situation where, if you don't realize it, you could potentially waste your time by making the same mistake. Learn from this so you don't continue to repeat the lesson.

No-Fail Rule # 5:
Prospects lie with fat words—Accept none of them.

You will hear "fat words" in response to the questions you ask throughout the entire sales process. These multiple-meaning words are ambiguous and often lead to different interpretations and conclusions between you and the prospect. Prospects have no problem lying to you because they don't think that lies to salespeople keep them out of heaven.

When you encounter fat words, simply say, "I don't understand," or "Help me understand what you mean by that" until you get all the information you need.

No-Fail Rule # 6:
"The truth and the money for me are at Level 3."

Uncover the real reasons why your prospects would change relationships, and determine if they're qualified. Drill down your questions until you hit the pain and get the truth or specifics of all the questions you ask.

You need to drill to at least the third level before prospects begin to tell you what you really need to know.

No-Fail Rule # 7:
Sell to prospects; teach customers.

Education is a vital part of any business; however, you become a teacher ONLY when the prospect becomes a customer. You get paid to secure and retain customers—not to be a teacher.

Your goal is to teach prospects only the following: the amount of pain they are experiencing by not being your customer and what all those pains are costing them. You are not there to help them understand how good their life could be with your company until they have told you how bad their life is without you.

183

Do not educate prospects on how you can fix their problem until they have told you they are committed to fixing their problem.

No-Fail Rule # 8:
Stop telling and start asking.

Prospects automatically make a connection between the size of your paycheck and how much "stuff" you're selling them. They naturally believe you get paid to talk them into changing their behavior.

Instead, take those same points you would like to tell them and ask questions about the concepts that lead to the same conclusion. By answering the questions, prospects take ownership of the answers and the associated consequences, thereby moving them from intellectually curious to economically serious.

No-Fail Rule # 9:
If you don't have a Unique Selling Proposition(s) (USP) and know where you get points for it in the evaluation and decision process, you lose.

You must have something the customer wants or values that sets you apart from the competition. This is your USP. Remember, your USP has to matter to your prospects—or it doesn't count. Make sure your prospects know what makes you different, and make sure they're willing to pay for it. This is the ONLY way to avoid a price war. Clarify with your prospects where and how you will get an advantage in their evaluation and decision process for having this USP. This is where you get your premium pricing.

No-Fail Rule # 10:
If you are not last in the beauty parade, you lose.

In a multi-vendor competition, you must be last. The final presenter will win the deal nine times out of ten.

184

What's next?

Congratulations! You now have a foolproof formula that can dramatically increase your income and the profitability of each sale you make. You have a leg-up on the competition and should feel empowered to make some BIG CHANGES.

For free chapter action plans to get you started, and for more information on how to better implement this process using accelerated learning tools filled with templates, tips, and strategies, visit www.EmmerichFinancial.com. Also, be sure to sign up for the free electronic newsletter to receive results-oriented strategies on sales, service, and business development.

This book is meant to be a practical guide that can lead you to huge breakthroughs. Remember, practice and repetition are the keys that will turn a new behavior into a habit. Don't give up! Keep going—and you will attain the results you desire.

If you've read this book in its entirety and are a highly motivated person who doesn't want to waste another minute presenting to unqualified prospects at the wrong time, then you are on the right track! Once you implement the information you have learned, you will start an extraordinary turnaround in your life.

- A mortgage lender from Ohio increased his production above his otherwise highest production month within thirty days of attending our Marketing and Sales Management Boot Camp.
- Many banks reported booking over 90 percent of loans that cleared credit committee—up from 30 percent on average.

- Investment representatives repeatedly tell stories of winning out against tough competitors in multi-million dollar deals.

If the Profit-Rich Sales System worked for them, it will also work for you (when you follow the sales process).

By following these rules and the simple step-by-step sales system revealed in this book, you will close more business at higher profit margins, have more free time (because the time you invest is more productive), and you will be far more respected by your prospects and clients. They will finally value your time as much as you do.

Review this book often, and constantly monitor your progress to make sure you are not forgetting any steps or rules during your calls. Any missteps will almost always cost you the business or the profit in the deal. Constant improvement and review are necessary for any top-performing athlete, scholar, or business person—and you are no exception.

Begin today to implement the Profit-Rich Sales System, and two things will happen: You will dramatically increase your sales and profits, AND you will notice that sales will never feel like selling again. What could be better than that?

Index

Help to Get You There Faster

To get started on creating a profit-rich transformation within your organization, visit www.EmmerichFinancial.com.

The site is loaded with implementation tools including free articles, templates, and action plans. While you're there, sign up for the FREE bi-monthly e-zine, which provides a steady stream of fresh marketing, sales, and leadership ideas to incite you and your colleagues to action.

And be sure to check out the descriptions of our most popular tools, designed to help you and your institution grow.

- *Profit-Rich Sales™ Seminar*
- *Profit-Rich Sales Management™ Seminar*
- *Profit-Rich Sales Trainer Certification™*
- *Marketing and Sales Management Boot Camp™*
- *Marketing and Sales Managementg Boot Camp II™*
- *Permission to Be Extraordinary™ Summit*
- *Train the Trainer™*
- *USP Development Seminar*
- *Breakthrough Banking™ Culture Development Program*
- *No More Order Taking™ Teleseminar System*

(Programs also available in packages.)

Call 800-236-5885 or e-mail Info@EmmerichGroup.com to learn more about the process that can best address—and transform—your unique situation.

Submit Your Success Stories

Please share with us your stories of success. Our staff is energized and excited by the breakthroughs of clients and readers alike; we all learn and grow through the experience of others. We want to hear about your experience-based ideas for the financial services industry—and how we can all improve the world of sales.

Contact us via e-mail: Info@EmmerichGroup.com

Or give us a call: 1-800-236-5885